In all Weathers!

50 inspiring ideas to enhance outdoor learning

The right of Sam Goddard to be identified as the author of this work has been asserted by him
in accordance with sections 77 and 78 of the Copyright, Designs and Patents Act 1988.

YD3031
ISBN 978-1-912758-00-5
© Sam Goddard
Photographs © Sam Goddard
All rights reserved
First published 2018
Printed in the UK for Yellow Door
PO Box 532, Cambridge, CB1 0BX, UK

Contents

Introduction

Why learn outdoors?

Before we explore the huge benefits of learning outdoors, it may be helpful to explain what we mean when we use the phrase 'outdoor learning'. In this book we use it as an umbrella term relating to any learning that takes place outside of a classroom or indoor space. Examples of such activities include outings and trips, sports, adventurous pursuits, child-led play, forest school sessions and learning through outdoor play.

All the activities in this book have been written to be accessible to every practitioner, regardless of level of training or degree of experience. They sit most comfortably under the outdoor learning definition above. Within the forest school movement, designated forest school practitioners need to be trained to Level 3 by an accredited training organisation in order to deliver its ethos effectively and undertake more challenging activities, such as lighting and using a fire, cooking and tool work. Such activities can be undertaken only by others with due diligence and following appropriate health and safety guidance. In this book, we have chosen to focus on activities that do not require such specialist training.

Working with young children is both a privilege and a big responsibility! We all want the children in our care to enjoy their learning and thrive in our settings. So the question is, how can outdoor learning help with this? To answer, we must first realise that outdoor learning is nothing new. Children have been learning outdoors, using their developing bodies and minds to make sense of the world around them, for thousands of years. However, there has been a decline in such involvement in the last few decades, with children spending more and more time indoors engaged in sedentary, technology-based activities or playing with machine-made toys and games. While there is nothing wrong with these types of activities in moderation, we need to be aware that children's brains are hardwired to engage with the natural world, and unless they are exposed to such relevant environments on a regular basis, we risk denying them the opportunities they need for optimal brain development.

Used appropriately by skilled practitioners, outdoor learning can:

Enhance coverage of the Early Years Foundation Stage in engaging and novel ways
The outdoors is the ultimate enabling environment. It is full of resources for open-ended play and learning, all subject to changing weather conditions and different seasons. It offers unique challenges and degrees of risk, as well as opportunities for understanding the world, and stimuli for literacy and maths. Once you get started, there are so many ways to cover the Early Years Foundation Stage (EYFS) outdoors!

Increase children's physical activity
Children's lack of physical activity is currently a big concern and Ofsted has highlighted it as something that needs to be prioritised in preschool settings. The outdoors is a tremendous place in which to run and climb, balance and swing. The great thing is that the children will be having such fun, they will not even realise they are exercising!

Improve specific skills and provide opportunities to develop lifelong learning interests
Some children need a chance to develop specific skills and help with focusing on a task. Through purposeful, rewarding outdoor activities, children can extend their concentration span, engage with their learning and start to develop interests that will stay with them for life.

Engage children in positive ways with their local natural environments
Children need to have an empathic relationship with natural environments nearby if they are to adopt a caring attitude towards nature. As Sir David Attenborough once said, 'No one will protect what they don't care about; and no one will care about what they have never experienced.'

Provide children with new opportunities to succeed
All humans are unique and have different skills and intelligences. The outdoor environment offers all children the chance to flourish and do something they are proud of.

Build practical skills, including appropriate risk taking
Outdoor learning lends itself to practical engagement and appropriate risk taking. Children need these opportunities in order to build their confidence, spatial awareness, physical strength and the ability to keep themselves safe in an ever-changing and unpredictable world.

Offer rewarding, purposeful, outcome-related activities
Provide children with a range of activities during outdoor sessions, so they can choose what interests them. In this way, the learning they are engaged in has personal relevance and will, therefore, be more rewarding and memorable.

Promote social skills
When busy outdoors, children tend to work in groups, take turns, share resources and collaborate more. These are all vital life skills that can be extended through outdoor learning. Next time you take a group of children outside, listen to the chatter that goes on; observe the negotiations, compromises and disagreements; and note down the social development taking place.

Build resilience, creativity and problem-solving skills
Things do not always work the first time outdoors, so children need to practise resilience. Open-ended tasks provide opportunities for problem solving and creativity. For example, supplying loose parts and small world figures is an excellent starting point for children's imaginative play.

Planning for outdoor learning
The first thing to say is that developing your outdoor learning provision should not create more work or add pressure to already busy workplaces! Outdoor learning is not another curriculum area that has to be delivered alongside all of your other commitments. Instead, it is a unique method of delivering your curriculum. To make the most of this approach, try including the outdoors on your existing planning template as a suitable context for covering the curriculum, and think of it in this way as you plan for your whole setting.

As you work on your medium-term planning, ask yourself, 'Could this area or outcome be delivered outside and, if so, how might I use the unique nature of the outdoors to enhance the children's learning?' As we have seen already, there are many areas of learning that can be delivered as well or better outdoors than inside. This is due to the nature of the outdoor environment and the way in which we plan children's experiences.

This book includes 50 complete outdoor learning sessions, one to two hours in duration. However, along with the structured activities, we also need to allow time for children to follow their own interests and engage in free play. This will allow them to deepen their

remember that in the early years, it is the process that is important, not the product. This is especially true of the outdoors. The real learning is in the exploring, doing, playing, and interacting that occurs.

There are many ways of encouraging this child-led learning approach outdoors. Several examples follow.
• Provide loose parts for physical play: tyres, planks, logs and rope.
• Use tarpaulins, coloured fabric and string to target enveloping schema, inviting the children to create spaces to play in.
• Build up a collection of natural materials for use during your outdoor sessions. Include shells, sticks, stones, cones and log slices. Observe how the children use these resources.
• Develop outdoor story sacks based on popular books, encouraging the children to explore them after having listened to the story outdoors.
• Provide natural messy-play resources, including mud, water, sand and soil, along with different containers and tools for the children to use for mixing, transporting and experimentation.
• Use a 'hook' or starting point to gain the children's interest and then let them develop and expand their ideas independently. For example, 'I wonder who lives here.', 'What's happened here?' or 'What's this I've found?'

Using the ideas in this book, along with free play and child-led learning, will provide your children with a wide range of meaningful, engaging and practical experiences outdoors. As practitioners, our job is to set the scene, provide the resources, give ideas for play and then step back and observe. Using familiar observational techniques will allow you to record and evaluate a child's learning, details of which can be added to their learning journey or profile. This process will help you to plan the next steps for each child going forwards and provide more meaningful and relevant experiences. Most of all, do not forget to enjoy the experience yourself!

The structure of an outdoor session
When you start engaging with outdoor learning, it is important to think about how you will structure your sessions to get the most from them. An outdoor session has a beginning, a middle and an end, with each section clearly defined and consistent, so the children become familiar with the structure. Outlined below are some ideas for the different elements of a session and what to include.

Develop a clearly defined space where you will gather each time you take a group of children for an outdoor learning session. This might be a log circle, seating area or just a space where you can stand together. Gathering in a circle allows everyone to see each other, which encourages good communication and focused listening.

Circle time and golden rules

At your gathering place, introduce the session and go through the golden rules for outdoor play. These need to be agreed with the children and should be simple and easy to remember. As you think about this, consider the following.

Set the boundaries

Which area are you using for your outdoor session and why?

Do you need to mark out this area to remind the children of the boundaries?

No pick, no lick!

This is to remind children not to pick things up and put them in their mouths. This is an important rule, especially with younger children. Get to know your site and check if you have any poisonous plants or fungi that you need to be aware of.

Carrying sticks

Talk to the children about how to safely carry sticks – either held vertically by their side or by dragging them along the ground if they are longer. Ask a child to demonstrate these methods to the rest of the group at the beginning of a session.

Litter

If there is a chance of the children finding litter on your site remind them never to touch it. Instead, they should tell you or an accompanying adult straightaway. It is useful to be specific about what you mean. For example, they can pick up a leaf but not a crisp packet or bottle. You could take some examples with you to show what you mean.

All back together!

It is a good idea to have a signal or call that the children recognise, which means 'Everyone back to the gathering place'. This could be a whistle, howl or bird call – be creative and make up your own! Once the children know what this means, practise using it on a regular basis to make sure they do not forget. You can then use this signal in the event of an emergency or just for when it is time to regroup.

If you have trees on your site, think about whether you will allow the children to climb them. With a risk assessment and safety procedure in place, tree climbing can be a really valuable physical play experience. However, you might want to set a height limit or select a specific tree to use.

Planning a session

Introduction

This is a way of starting a session and allowing the children to explore the site. Each of the 50 activities in this book has an introductory activity linked to the theme, but feel free to mix and match these, or even make up your own. The children will be excited to explore the site, so it is a good idea to have an activity that gives a reason to do this.

Main activity

This is the main body of your session and will probably include one or more structured, adult-led activities or experiences for the children to take part in if and when they want to. Remember, outdoor learning is about the process not the product, so do not get too hung up on all the children taking part; some might prefer to follow their own ideas instead. The main activities in this book can be roughly divided into the following types:

• Sensory
• Imaginative/Role play
• Mud play
• Water play
• Story/Music
• Physical
• Creative
• Construction.

Extension

As part of the main activity always try to allow time for the children to extend and develop their learning by providing opportunities and resources for extension. This is when child-led learning comes into its own. It is ultimately the children who will come up with the best ideas. Have a back-up collection of open-ended resources on hand to offer the children to aid their thinking. For example, after a story about the three bears, having some soft toy bears available would be a good way of extending the play.

Leave time for some free play in your outdoor sessions. Provide resources, if necessary, or allow the children to explore the world around them. This is a great time to record some observations!

Reflections

The final part of a session is a chance to reflect. This is often, but not always, done at your gathering place and can take the form of a quiet or dynamic activity. This is hugely valuable for the children and any adults involved. It helps to deepen the learning and gives a sense of what the group enjoyed so you can work this into your next session. Each of this book's 50 activities includes a reflective activity, but, again, feel free to mix these up or develop your own.

Links to EYFS

Each of the 50 activities includes a section indicating specific links to the Early Learning Goals (ELGs) of the EYFS. If an ELG is built into the structure of all the activities, we have not shown it. This specifically relates to:
• Communicating and language: Understanding (ELG 02)
• Personal, social and emotional development: Self-confidence and Self-awareness (ELG 06).

Risk assessment as an enabling tool

When we accompany children outdoors to learn, it can take them outside of their comfort zone and ours as practitioners, too! Many working in Early Years settings are worried about real and perceived risks that are present when children are active outdoors, and this can be one of the main barriers to settings developing an integrated approach to outdoor learning.

This book is full of lots of practical ideas to enhance and extend children's learning by using the special nature of the great outdoors. Some of these activities come with an element of risk. There is a good reason for this – unless children are given opportunities to explore risk in a supported way during their early years, they may find it more difficult to assess risk and keep themselves safe as they grow up. Risk assessment is a life skill that we use every day, from walking down a busy street to climbing some stairs. We need to give children the opportunities to explore risk and participate in activities that involve an element of age and/or developmentally-appropriate risk.

a tree. During this activity, they are engaging their gross motor skills and developing muscle use. They are becoming more spatially aware and learning about the properties of the world around them. Social skills will develop as the child communicates with others, talking about how they are climbing. A child who is a proficient climber could help their less confident peers, enhancing their emotional literacy and giving them a sense of responsibility and purpose. None of these benefits would be available if we simply said tree climbing is too dangerous!

The process of risk assessment helps to make us aware of the potential hazards an activity presents and gives us the means to reduce any risk to a level we are comfortable with. To emphasise, the risk needs to be reduced to a level where it is appropriate rather than removed altogether. As the Health and Safety executive states – environments for children need to be made as safe as necessary, not as safe as possible (www.hse.gov.uk/services/education/sensible-leadership/index.htm).

Below is a risk/benefit process that we find helpful in our own planning.
1. Decide on the activity and think about all the amazing benefits the children will gain from it. This is the fun part! Use your knowledge of the children as well as the EYFS for this.

2. Identify any potential hazards. A hazard is anything that might cause harm, which could range from a branch on the ground to a piece of string used in the planned activity. This is best done outdoors, preferably at the site you are going to use for the activity, so you can get a feel for any potential hazards.

3. Consider who might be harmed by any hazards, and how. For example, a piece of string could harm a child or adult by getting tangled around their neck or fingers causing a burn, or through ingestion. Be realistic, there is no need to invent risks!

4. Decide what you are going to do about this hazard. We call this a control. Is it a high enough risk to remove it altogether or could you highlight it with some sort of visual marker? Perhaps all you need to do is to make the children aware of how to manage a risk. For example, if a tree branch is hanging over your gathering place, you are probably going to want to avoid that area until it has been dealt with by a qualified tree surgeon. On the other hand, some stinging nettles in the corner of your site will probably

be best dealt with by showing the children where they are and warning them not to touch them without wearing gloves. You can involve the children in this process, asking for their thoughts and ideas on what level a risk might pose and how it might be dealt with. You might be surprised at how sensible their suggestions are!

5. Decide who is going to carry out any control, and when. Put a name against the task, making any action specific and agree a timescale for the work, making a record when it has been resolved.

6. Having carried out your control actions, review the consequent level of risk. Balance this against the benefits you noted at the start. The idea is that the benefits now outweigh any potential risks. If they do not, go back and revisit your control methods.

Taken together, the above steps should enable you to carry out all of the activities in this book, and lots more. We are responsible for the opportunities the children in our care have and we must ensure that, while being safe, these opportunities are rich, varied and challenging in order to enable children to flourish in our wonderful outdoor environments!

Curious collectors

As we know, children love collecting. This is such a natural activity that sometimes all we need to do is provide them with an opportunity and they will begin collecting with little further input! Below are some ideas of how you can capitalise on the pleasure of collecting.

Starter

Gather lots of different containers and keep them with your outdoor resources. Having a variety of sizes and shapes of container will allow for different collecting opportunities. Try the following: yogurt pots, egg boxes, matchboxes, cotton drawstring bags, mini-buckets or trugs, baskets, camera film pots, paper bags, and so on.

Allow each child to choose a container and go on a collecting expedition. After a while, gather the children and explore what they have in their containers, asking why they picked one or two of the items.

Resources

• Strips of card with pieces of double-sided tape attached
• Gloves may be useful.

Main activity

Give each child a sticky strip of card to use to create a collection. At first allow them to decide what they want to collect. However, if you repeat this activity, set each child a focus: colour, texture, sound, smell, and so on. You may want to ask the children to create a picture of an outdoor scene, make a repeating pattern or collect a specific number of objects. The possibilities are endless!

This activity works best on a dry day. On a wet one, the collections soon fall off the cards.

Extension ideas

• Wrap the strip of card to create a looped nature bracelet.
• Use longer strips of card to make nature crowns.
• Play a collecting game: shout a colour that the children must find an example of to stick onto their strip as quickly as they can. Try other themes too.

• Develop mathematical thinking: start a pattern on a card and challenge a group of children to continue it by collecting the relevant objects and sticking them on the strip.
• Collect each colour of the rainbow on a separate strip of card, then arrange the cards to represent a rainbow.

Reflections

Ask the children to make a picture each by attaching objects to sticky strips of card to show what they enjoyed or found challenging about the session. Ask them to explain the picture to a friend. With younger children, this can be done with adult support.

Links to EYFS

• Physical development: Moving and handling (ELG 04)
• Understanding the world: The world (ELG 14).

Follow your nose

> Children's sensory development continues through their early years, with outdoor spaces being ideal environments to assist with this. This activity focuses on the sense of smell, using natural and introduced objects as stimuli.

Starter

Invite the children to close their eyes and gently sniff the air of your outdoor space. Explore the following questions.

• What can you smell?
• Are there any particular smells you can identify?
• What words describe what you are smelling? (Examples may be damp, musty, stinky, fresh, and so on.)

Develop this theme by going on a smell walk around your site. Lead the children, stopping by anything with an interesting aroma, asking them to describe what they smell. Record their suggestions so as to build up a word bank of descriptive language.

Resources

• Reusable plastic cups
• Small sticks
• Smelly items (see below)
• Water.

Main activity

Give each child a cup and challenge them to collect items from your outdoor area that have interesting smells. It is a good idea to set some limits on what they can pick up, avoiding human-made litter, for example. Once the children have finished, pour some water into each child's cup to mix their items with, stirring their potion with a small stick.

Encourage the children to share their smelly potions with each other, exploring which mixture's smell they find the most appealing or revolting. Who has the smelliest potion of all?

Remember to emphasise that these potions are not for drinking!

You could augment the natural objects with others from beyond your outdoor area, such as:

• Fresh herbs: rosemary, thyme, sage
• Spices: cinnamon, cumin, clove
• Coffee grounds
• Onion
• Banana
• Mint toothpaste
• Essential oils.

Extension ideas

• Add other items to the potions to change how they look, such as food colouring and biodegradable glitter.
• Make a 'smelly bag' by placing cotton wool soaked in an aromatic liquid in a cotton bag for the children to smell. Repeat with other liquids to provide a selection.
• Create a 'smelly card' by sticking strips of double-sided tape on a piece of card. Challenge the children to collect smelly items from the setting and stick them to their card.

Reflections

At the end of the session, give each child an opportunity to talk about the smells they found. They might describe their favourite smell, make up a name for this smell or talk about other smells they can think of, good or bad.

Links to EYFS

• Mathematics: Shape, space and measures (ELG 12)
• Understanding the world: The world (ELG 14).

Outdoor explorers

It is important that children feel familiar with, safe in and connected to the outdoor environment. This is achieved most effectively by ensuring they have frequent and long-term access to the natural world. When you go outdoors, it is vital that the children are given the chance to explore the site and really get to know what is there.

Starter

When you visit a new site with a group of children, make sure they have plenty of time to explore it. This will be more natural for some than others, depending on their previous experience of playing outdoors. If some children are reluctant to leave an adult, play a game to encourage them to explore on their own. Hide-and-seek games are great for this. If some children find such games difficult, hide with them, building up slowly to them hiding independently.

Resources

• Binoculars
• Telescopes
• Magnifying glasses
• Rolled-up card tubes
• Camera
• Backpacks or collecting bags.

Main activity

Take some of the above equipment with you to your outdoor area, explaining that today the children are going to be explorers. Magnifying glasses, binoculars and telescopes help children get a different perspective on the world around them. Create a story to help the children to explore the site. They can be tiny ants looking for a nice green leaf, explorers searching for a lost city or pirates surveying the oceans.

If you have backpacks for the children, these can add to the excitement and give them somewhere to put their equipment and any interesting finds. Take photographs of any exciting discoveries. Ask the children to make up stories about what they have found and tell them to the others in the group. For example, a big log might be part of a dinosaur skeleton or a shipwrecked boat!

Extension ideas

• Tell a story about someone making a discovery to inspire the children.
• This is a great opportunity for free play, so allow the activity to evolve.
• Make 'log dogs' as pets for the children to take exploring with them. Tie a piece of string around a log so that the children can lead it around the site.
• Use the stories and games that come out of this activity to inspire more learning and play indoors and outside. For example, if the children find a pirate ship, planning more pirate-based activities will extend this theme.

Reflections

Ask the children to tell a short story or give an account of where they went when they were exploring, and what they saw. This can be presented to the whole group or a selection of friends. Adult support may be needed by younger children.

Links to EYFS

• Personal, social and emotional development: Making relationships (ELG 08)
• Understanding the world: The world (ELG 14).

Tracks and trails

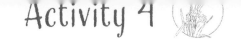

Using tracks and trails to explore an outdoor setting works very well. It can also encourage nervous children to venture away from adults to visit parts of the site they may not have been to before.

Starter
Prepare by setting up a trail leading to the area you are going to use. Allow the children to find the trail, and their natural curiosity will prompt them to follow it! A flour trail works well as it stands out on the ground and is easy to follow. Other alternatives include a rope trail, a map or a line of directional arrows.

Resources
• Rope
• Blindfolds
• Magnifying glasses
• Paper and pencils
• Mud
• Water
• Buckets, guttering and hosepipes
• Coloured chalks
• Charcoal.

Main activity
When the children reach the destination, there are lots of tracking activities they might do. Here are some favourites:
• Set up rope trails taking in different areas of your site for the children to follow while blindfolded. Tie objects on the rope at different points for them to explore with their remaining senses.
• Pretend to be tiny ants and look for small trails to follow on the ground, using magnifying glasses to examine finds in more detail, drawing any discoveries.
• Make wellie boot trails through mud, and then run on tarmac or paving slabs to make a trail of footprints.
• Make trails with water on a dry day, or move rain using guttering, hosepipes and buckets on a wet one.
• Draw arrows on trees using coloured chalks and charcoal leading to some 'treasure' or a hidden child.
• Make maps using mud and charcoal. Encourage the children to use their fingers to mark trails. They are great as paintbrushes!

Extension ideas
• Hide 'treasure' in a muddy area for the children to dig up.
• Give flour to the children so that they can lay their own trails when playing Hide and Seek.
• Go on a scavenger hunt for natural objects from your outdoor area.

Reflections
As you have been thinking about hiding and finding things, you could ask the children if they have ever been lost. Discuss what they would do in this circumstance, and who they might ask for help. This is a valuable opportunity for children to talk about the feelings they have had when lost, as well as a chance to give them some practical guidance on how to keep safe in such a situation. For example, not going off with anyone they do not know.

Links to EYFS
• Personal, social and emotional development: Managing feelings and behaviour (ELG 07)
• Understanding the world: The world (ELG 14).

Adopt a tree

If you have some trees in your outdoor area or nearby make the most of this wonderful resource by spending time getting to know them. Children need to feel a sense of connection with the natural world, which we can facilitate by giving them the opportunity to familiarise themselves with their local trees.

Starter

Make a leaf lucky dip by placing leaves collected from your outdoor area in a bag. You can use fresh leaves, dried leaves that have been pressed or laminated ones, which will last longer. You will need enough leaves to ensure no-one is left out. When each child has taken a leaf from the lucky dip, tell them that the leaves are lost and need to find their way home. Challenge the children to find the parent tree of their leaf. Such careful observation is the start of being able to identify trees and plants.

Resources

• Blindfolds
• Card/Paper
• Charcoal.

Main activity

Once each child has found their tree, they are going to adopt it for the rest of the session. It is now their tree.

Ask the children to sit by their adopted trees for a couple of minutes in order to experience what it feels like to do so. If they close their eyes, they may be able to hear nearby sounds, imagining what their tree can hear. As an extension, ask the children to find their tree while blindfolded.

Invite the children to investigate their trees using their senses. Allow them to explore the tree with their hands while blindfolded, feeling the bark's texture and the shape of the trunk. Ask them to complete the sentence, 'I touched my tree and it felt like …'. Repeat the activity, adapting the sentence for smell, sight and sound.

The children could draw their trees using charcoal or chalks, taking the results back to the setting to create a display. You may want to video the children talking about their trees to use as evidence of their learning.

Extension ideas

• Conduct minibeast hunts around the trees to help the children learn more about the creatures that live nearby.
• Catch any insects or bugs living in foliage by shaking branches in turn over a white sheet. Be careful not to damage the tree.
• Encourage the children to build mini-homes for the creatures they discover in/on their trees, or for an imaginary animal that lives in the area.
• Regularly return to the same trees to see what has changed. Doing this will build a connection between each child and their tree.

Reflections

Ask the children to sit under their tree quietly and reflect on what it has seen and heard in its lifetime. Can they guess how old their tree might be?

Make up a story as a group about what has happened around the trees during their long lives. Perhaps they have witnessed battles, seen kings, queens, outlaws, and so on.

Links to EYFS

• Personal, social and emotional development: Managing feelings and behaviour (ELG 07)
• Understanding the world: The world (ELG 14).

The outdoors is a fantastic environment in which to explore sound and music. Children can be more vocal, noisy and expressive when they are not constrained by the four walls of an indoor space. Allow children to have plenty of opportunities to make loud noises, shout and let off steam when outside.

Starter

Ask the children to find a stick each and tell them they are going to be sound detectives. Explain that the object of the activity is to find things that make a really interesting sound when hit with a stick. The children can hunt individually or in small groups. At the end of the activity, listen to the sounds of the objects found and discuss what makes a good sound. You can record the sounds on an iPad or sound recorder to take indoors for later use.

Resources

• Donated kitchen items
• Sticks
• Rope
• Logs.

Main activity

Create your own sound wall or sculpture in your outdoor area. This can be a very low-cost activity if you obtain objects from parents/carers or source them from charity shops. Good items to look for include pots, pans, colanders, metal oven racks and plastic tubes – any objects that make a good noise when bashed!

Find a fence or tree and tie the items you have collected to it. Cut some straight sticks and keep them in a box near your sound wall for the children to use to experiment with.

You can make a wooden xylophone by hanging fairly chunky logs securely from a branch for the children to play. Seasoned wood works best for this, and you may need to cut the logs to different lengths to create a variety of notes.

Extension ideas

• Collect some fallen leaves. Explore how many different sounds the children make with them. Try crunching, rubbing and tearing.

• Invite the children to shut their eyes and imagine they are in a world full of sounds. What can they hear in this imagined world? What might be making the sounds?
• Whisper rhymes and then shout them as loud as possible. Can the children wake the local animals?
• Make natural shakers. Take two reusable cups and fill one with objects collected from your outdoor area. Tape the cups together open end to open end and shake!

Reflections

Being quiet and still is a skill to be practised, so encourage silent reflection at the end of the session with a calming activity. Ask the children to find a quiet place to sit or lie down. You could cover the children with leaves if they are happy with this, so that they become part of the woodland floor. Ask them to listen to see if they can hear from which direction sounds are coming from. When they hear a sound, ask them to point in the direction they think it came from. Allow time for discussion before ending the activity.

Links to EYFS

• Expressive arts and design: Exploring and using media and materials (ELG 16)
• Expressive arts and design: Being imaginative (ELG 17).

Marks and maps

Maps can be tricky for younger children to decipher, but simpler versions can help to create a sense of place and enable children to explore representing the world using symbols. Begin with simple maps and build up to more complex ones as the children's confidence grows.

Starter

Give each child a length of coloured ribbon to indicate an area in the outdoor space that they find exciting, interesting or good for adventures. When they have discovered such a spot, they need to find a suitable place to attach their ribbon as a marker. Once completed, allow time for each child to tell the others about their special place and why they chose it.

Resources

• Large tarpaulin or sheet
• Natural materials
• Small world figures.

Main activity

Lay out a large tarpaulin or sheet to represent a map of your outdoor area. Mark some features to help the children visualise the area: buildings, fences, and so on. Ask the children to explore where their special places are on the map. If this is too much of a challenge, they can point to where they would like to put their special place instead. You could provide resources for the children to build a model of their special place on the map. For example, sticks for the log circle, twigs for the trees and stones for the paths. Once the map is finished, invite the children to show a small world figure or soft toy around the area, explaining the key features.

Extension ideas

• Ask the children to create a map of an imaginary landscape or somewhere they have visited.
• Draw on card with charcoal to create smaller maps.
• Make journey cards by sticking collected objects from around your site onto strips of card to indicate the journey taken for others.
• Make a map of a story (See We're Going on a Bear Hunt, page 49).

Reflections

This is a quiet activity during which the children sit for a moment with a small piece of card and a pencil or piece of charcoal. Ask them to make a mark when they hear a sound, and discuss what it might be or where it might be coming from. For slightly older children, they could draw what they think is making the sound or a visual representation of it: a wavy line for wind in the trees or a spiky line for a passing lorry. This is a great activity for encouraging concentration and focus, and can be really soothing at the end of a busy session.

Links to EYFS

• Mathematics: Shape, space and measures (ELG 12)
• Expressive arts and design: Exploring and using media and materials (ELG 16).

Wonderful wind

Standing in an open field or meadow on a windy day may be something that the children have not experienced before, and is a wonderful sensation and learning opportunity. This activity should not be conducted underneath mature trees due to the possibility of falling branches.

Starter
Begin a windy session by inviting each child to imagine standing on their own magic carpet, letting the wind blow them to the outdoor area. Model big 'windy' movements: rotating your arms to mimic being blown along by the wind.

At your gathering place, discuss the wind using the questions below.
• How does the wind make you feel?
• How is it different to being outdoors on a still day?
• What effects is the wind having? (trees swaying, leaves blowing, people's hair ruffling)

Ask the children to close their eyes and feel the wind on their face. Invite them to tell you a word that describes what it feels like.

Resources
• String
• Sticks
• Long pieces of wool and/or ribbon
• Elastic bands.

Main activity
Ask the children to look around the outdoor area for things that move in the wind. You can make suggestions or allow the children to decide what they will collect. Encourage them to think about the properties of the objects and why these might cause them to move in the wind.

Once the children have collected some objects, create a group wind sculpture. Attach the objects onto pieces of string and suspend them from a branch or similar. The result will be a curtain of the collected objects fluttering in the wind! Experiment with adding heavier objects, observing how they move.

Finally, give out the pieces of wool or ribbon, along with other lightweight collected objects. Fix these onto the end of a stick using string or elastic bands. In this way each child will create a natural streamer that they can run around with in the wind – a great way to get some physical exercise!

Extension ideas
• Throw leaves in the air and watch them blow in the wind. Can the children catch a leaf, making a wish when they have done so?
• Flick watered-down paint onto some paper from a distance and watch the effect the wind has on it.
• Decorate a tree with ribbons, wool and other objects to make a 'wind tree' and watch it move.

Reflections
As this is a physical activity, you may find it difficult to get the children to reflect quietly at the end of it. So try some loud reflections instead!

Stand in a circle and pass an object from one child to the next. When each child has the object, they can shout a word that describes how they felt about the session as loudly as they can into the wind. You can explore whether an adult standing downwind can hear the word.

Links to EYFS
• Personal, social and emotional development: Managing feelings and behaviour (ELG 07)
• Understanding the world: The world (ELG 14).

Rain doctors

A rainy day is an opportunity not to be missed! The sounds, smells and sights of a downpour of rain can be really exciting, providing lots of opportunities for sensory development. If you can, put up a shelter sheet or tarpaulin on a really wet day so you and the children have somewhere to stay dry and listen to the rain.

Starter

During a heavy downpour, take a small tarpaulin outside and ask the children to space out and hold on to its edges, drawing it off the ground, and creating a dip in the middle where the rain will pool. You will need some adults to help make sure it stays off the ground. See if the group can keep the water on the tarpaulin without it spilling over the edges.

This is a great activity to encourage teamwork and cooperation as it requires the whole group to work together for it to be successful.

This activity can be done on a dry day by bringing your own water outside, but it works best when it is wet.

Resources
• Rain box resources (see below)

Main activity
If you are lucky enough to have a day of rain, provide lots of loose parts for the children to use to explore this natural resource. You could put together a rain box including some of the following items:
• Lengths of hose
• 1 metre lengths of guttering and down pipe
• Children's umbrellas
• Funnels
• Jugs
• Buckets
• Basins
• Spray bottles
• Sieves/Colanders
• Watering cans.

These can be used variously to catch the rain, put it into containers, transport it and explore how it moves. Use the guttering and tubes to make your own water installation by connecting them to a fence or wall and allowing the children to explore the way the water flows. This can be a temporary piece or you can leave it for future rainy days.

Extension ideas
• Make music by catching raindrops in different containers and investigating what noises they make. Encourage the children to use as many receptacles as they can and listen for the differences in sound.
• Use umbrellas to dance in the rain!
• Dig a big hole and fill it with water. Challenge the children to make a bridge across it that they can walk over using planks of wood.

Reflections
Sit under a tree's canopy in the rain with the children. All close your eyes and listen to the sound of the rain on the leaves and branches. Talk about how it feels to be sheltering under the tree. What can the children say about what they can see and hear, and how they feel?

Links to EYFS
• Personal, social and emotional development: Managing feelings and behaviour (ELG 07)
• Understanding the world: The world (ELG 14).

Puddle professors

> Sometimes rain is used as an excuse for not going outdoors rather than a fantastic learning opportunity! As the old saying goes, 'There is no such thing as bad weather, just bad clothing.' Make sure all participants are dressed in warm, waterproof clothing and then head out to experience all types of weather, including rain.

Starter

Go on a puddle hunt, asking:
• Who can find the biggest puddle?
• Are there any places where puddles are more common?
• Why do you think the puddles have formed in these places?
• How do puddles form on different surfaces? Why do you think this is?
• What can you see in the puddles? Can anyone spot a reflection?

You might see a rainbow effect in a puddle if any oil has mixed with the water, or there may be tiny creatures living in larger puddles!

Measure the depth and width of puddles using a metre stick. Allow the children to try to jump over the puddles.

Resources

• Floating/Sinking objects (see below)
• Chalk
• Elastic bands
• Dry wood – this floats the best.

Main activity

Take a variety of objects to a nice big puddle for a floating/sinking experiment. Good items to take include:
• Corks
• Feathers
• Stones
• Small flat pieces of wood
• Marbles
• Plastic yogurt pots
• Clay.

Ask the children to predict which objects will float or sink, using the following questions when conducting the experiment:
• Which object made the biggest splash? Why do you think that was?
• If we are gentle with how we put things in the water, will they still make a splash?
• What happens after something has been dropped in? (Talk about ripples and how the circles get bigger until they disappear.)

With older groups, ask the children to sort the objects into two groups: 'floaters' and 'sinkers'. Once tested, use two hoops or chalk circles to sort the objects into.

Make model boats using corks, matchsticks and collected objects. It is easy to fix them together using clay or elastic bands. Explore the properties that a boat needs to make it float. This can be a stand-alone session, with the children working on their boat designs indoors and/or outdoors.

Extension ideas

• Draw around puddles with chalk, revisiting them to see if they have grown or shrunk.
• Have a boat race. Set a start and an end point, and release the boats to see which ones make it to the end.
• Splash in puddles, exploring who can make the biggest splash. Measure how far the water splashes from the original puddle.

Reflections

Sit as a group underneath a tarpaulin or shelter in the rain. Listen to the sounds the raindrops make on the covering and ask the children to describe them. Talk about how it feels to be in the dry with the rain falling all around. What can the children say about what they see and hear under the shelter, and how they feel?

Links to EYFS

• Personal, social and emotional development: Managing feelings and behaviour (ELG 07)
• Mathematics: Shape, space and measures (ELG 12)
• Understanding the world: The world (ELG 14).

Mud is a wonderful, free resource that is safe, sustainable and easily accessible. Why would we not make use of it? When you do, make sure that children are suitably dressed: full waterproofs and wellies are best, and do not forget the hand-washing kit!

Starter

Challenge the children to find the biggest, muddiest area in your setting. If there is not much mud, you can bring some soil in from elsewhere and mix it with water to make your own.

Encourage the children to stamp in the mud and tell the group what it feels like. You can even suggest they take their wellies and socks off to feel the mud between their toes! Make sure you carry out a risk assessment before trying this.

Roll a long piece of paper out – wallpaper works well – and invite the children to run or walk along it, making lots of lovely muddy footprints. This makes a wonderful display, if you can rescue it before it disintegrates!

Resources

- Mud
- Water
- Spades
- Trowels
- Collected natural materials – lots of different colours and shapes
- Hand-washing kit.

Main activity

Spades and trowels are great for using with mud, and are a good addition to any outdoor area. Use the spades to mix some mud with water to make a smooth, thick paste roughly the consistency of play dough. This can be used like clay to make all sorts of fantastic creations! Here are some ideas:

- Mud hedgehogs – shape mud into a ball and push sticks in it for the spines
- Mud snakes – roll out a coil of mud and decorate it with natural materials
- Mud faces – push a mud ball onto a tree trunk, adding eyes, nose and mouth made of sticks, leaves and feathers
- Mud minibeasts – create a mud bug, using sticks for the legs and wings.

Extension ideas

- Encourage the children to jump in muddy puddles in order to see who can make the biggest splash!
- Make a mud slide down a small hill. Dig out a channel and pour water into it for the children to slide down. WARNING: this is a very muddy activity!
- Add different resources to your mud kitchen to encourage imaginative play.
- Invite the children to dip their hands in wet mud and make handprints on paper or trees.
- Use the mud like face paint to create scary monsters or animals!

Reflections

Mud can be used for reflective activities too. The children could paint a mud picture using their fingers or a paintbrush, perhaps a self-portrait or something they did that day. Once they have finished, they could find a friend and show them what they have done.

Links to EYFS

- Understanding the world: The world (ELG 14)
- Expressive arts and design: Exploring and using media and materials (ELG 16).

Happy habitats

Looking in detail at your outdoor area is a skill that you and your children can develop together. It is also a first step towards identifying developments that will make it more wildlife friendly. Ways of assessing your area may include minibeast hunts, species identification and finding out what other plants and animals live nearby.

Starter

Talk with your group about the word 'habitat'.
• What do you think this word means?
• Why do you think good habitats are important for animals?
• What dangers are there if there is no habitat for a particular animal?

Go on a minibeast hunt or do some pond dipping, if you are lucky enough to have a pond nearby. Identify your finds and take photographs of them to compile a record of the minibeasts you have at your site already. You could make a pictogram or graph of the different species.

Resources

• Soil
• Collected materials
• Plastic or foil trays – unused cat litter trays work well.

Main activity

Revisit the theme of habitats, asking the children what ones they can spot in your outdoor area. Examples might include a grassy area, an old rotten log, a tree or a pond. Discuss which creatures live in these habitats and what makes the habitats particularly suitable for them.

Encourage the children to have a go at building habitats suitable for some of the minibeasts they found. Give out foil or plastic trays filled with soil. Ask the children to make mini-habitats based on ones they have found or imagined. They could include stones, mud, water, plants, and so on. The nice thing about using trays is that the habitats can be moved, so you can position them in your outdoor area or even take them indoors as a display. Just make sure there are no real creatures living in them before you do!

Extension ideas

• Make larger habitats for creatures that may live in your outdoor area: mice, foxes, owls, garden birds.
• Tie together small lengths of bamboo with wool to make habitats for solitary bees to hibernate in.
• Make habitats for imaginary creatures using the same technique.

Reflections

Give out magnifying glasses and ask the children to imagine what it would be like to be a minibeast. Ask them to get down on all fours and use their magnifiers to investigate the ground close up, describing what they see. You could pretend to shrink them with a magic ray! Ask the children to talk about how it felt to be so small and how it might feel for the minibeasts you have looked at.

Links to EYFS

• Understanding the world: The world (ELG 14)
• Expressive arts and design: Exploring and using media and materials (ELG 16).

Busy birds

This is a great activity for the spring when birds are becoming more active. Foster the children's curiosity by watching the birds with them and asking what they notice them doing at this exciting time of the year.

Starter
Introduce this activity by asking the children what they notice about the changing seasons.
- What is happening outdoors that is new?
- What signs of new life can you see?
- What are the birds doing at the moment?

Such questions will help you to find out what the children know and how you may need to adapt the activities. You may want to go on a bird hunt, and even, perhaps, find some nests.

Resources
- Dry grass
- Straw
- Moss
- Feathers
- Twigs
- Sticks.

Main activity
Mini-nests
Using natural materials such as the above, challenge the children to make mini-nests for the birds they spotted. Discuss the characteristics of a good nest. Does it need to be soft or hard, up high or down low, big or small? Discuss how birds make their nests with their beaks. Ask the children how having fingers make it easier/harder to build a mini-nest.

Use small round stones or marbles as eggs, or make your own using clay.

Giant nest
Ask every child to find a stick as long as their arm. They can pretend to be birds and fly off to gather their sticks. Once everyone has returned, form a circle. Ask the children to stand and hold their sticks in front of them horizontally as if holding bicycle handlebars. Reduce the size of the circle until the sticks touch end to end. Place the sticks on the

ground to create a circular outline of a giant nest. Now it is over to the children – your flock of birds – to gather as many sticks as they can to build up the walls of the nest making it nice and cosy!

You may want to provide a guide for younger children by marking out the shape of the giant nest on the ground with rope.

Extension ideas
- Add toy birds to the mini-nests to use in small world play.
- Decorate the giant nest with coloured feathers, dry grass, straw and other natural materials.

Reflections
Sit in the giant nest together and talk about how it feels.
- What words describe how you feel in the nest?
- If you were a bird, what else would you need to survive?

This can lead nicely on to other activities, such as making bird feeders or putting up bird boxes.

Links to EYFS
- Physical development: Moving and handling (ELG 04)
- Understanding the world: The world (ELG 14)
- Mathematics: Shape, space and measures (ELG 12).

Woolly worms

This activity explores camouflage and how some animals use it to keep themselves safe. Begin by looking at some pictures of worms and other minibeasts with the children. Discuss the colours and shapes of the creatures and the possible reasons for them.

Starter

Conduct an outdoor colour hunt. You may want to give the children different pieces of coloured card to match to. Paint sample cards from DIY stores work well. Ask the children why they think some colours are harder to spot than others. Which colours do they think are the most common in your outdoor area? This can vary depending on the time of year, so it is worth repeating this activity regularly.

Resources

• Lots of pieces of coloured wool – some bright and some more natural colours
• A stick
• Cards with strips of double-sided tape attached.

Main activity

While you are talking with the group about the colours they have found, another adult needs to hide lots of short pieces of coloured wool in easy-to-reach places around the site. The wool pieces need to be roughly the length of a worm.

Explain to the children that they are going to be baby birds that need to fly off to find some tasty worms for their dinner. Show them a woolly worm and explain that no worms – real or woolly – are to be eaten during this activity. Once a woolly worm has been found, they are to give it to you or another adult – the mummy or daddy bird – and then fly off to find another.

Tie the woolly worms to a stick or place them on the sticky card as you receive them, creating a tally of the colours collected and in what order. The brighter colours are usually found first, with the more natural shades being harder to spot.

This activity also works with coloured lolly sticks or pipe cleaners.

Extension ideas

• Introduce an element of competition, with two teams vying to find the most worms. Use a hoop on the ground for each team to put their worms in.
• Denote one colour of worm as poisonous – red works well. Tell the children to avoid these worms.
• Minibeast hunts can extend this activity, with a focus on which colours the children need to look for.

Reflections

At the end of the activity, gather together and ask the children about the experience.
• How did it feel?
• How difficult/easy was it to find the worms? Why was that the case?
• Which colours were easier/trickier to spot?

Look at the woolly worm tally.
• Which worms were found first/last?
• Why do you think this was the case?

This is a good time to introduce the term 'camouflage' and explain what it means. Ask the children what colour they would like to be if they were a worm trying to avoid being caught!

Links to EYFS

• Personal, social and emotional development: Managing feelings and behaviour (ELG 07)
• Mathematics: Shape, space and measures (ELG 12)
• Understanding the world: The world (ELG 14).

Marvellous minibeasts

Minibeasts are fascinating creatures, which makes searching for them a really valuable learning experience for children. As the children get older, introducing the names, characteristics and varieties of minibeasts will deepen their understanding.

Starter

Explain to the children that they are going to pretend to be a family of ants following a trail home. It is better to have an adult as the lead ant for the first few games. When they find something of interest on the path, they pick it up and pass it back over their head to the ant behind. The ant that received the object passes it over their head and waits for it to reach the back of the line. When it has, the last ant runs to the front of the line and the game continues.

This is an excellent activity for practising gross motor skills, coordination and collaboration.

Resources
• Minibeast collecting kits
• Spoons
• White tray
• Laminated pictures of minibeasts.

Main activity

Discuss the creatures the children might find living in your outdoor area. Look at pictures of likely insects so the group know what to look for. Give out the collecting kits and encourage the children, with adult help, to look for minibeasts and try to identify what they find. Explain that any insects the children find will need to be treated with respect.

When a child finds a minibeast, they may study it and show it to the group. It is a good idea to collect any minibeasts in a tray, enabling the children to observe how they move, before returning them to their natural habitat.

Lay the pictures of insects on the ground, placing a stone on the relevant image each time a creature is found. This tally can be used to find out what is the most common minibeast in your outdoor area.

Extension ideas
• Observe minibeasts and draw them on paper with charcoal.
• Ask the children to move like minibeasts. They can mime a given creature or choose their own. The rest of the group must try to guess the minibeast from their movements.
• Make mud models of minibeasts. Use a ball of mud for the body, and sticks/leaves for legs and wings.
• Create butterfly art by painting a butterfly wing on one half of a piece of paper, which is folded over onto the blank half. When unfolded, a full butterfly outline will be revealed.

Reflections

Ask the children which minibeast they think is best suited to living in their local natural environment, and why.

Discuss what sorts of minibeast the children would like to invent.

Links to EYFS
• Understanding the world: The world (ELG 14).

Once you have been on a minibeast hunt with the children (see page 22), extend the learning by building simple habitats for the creatures they found.

Starter
Refresh what was learned during the minibeast hunt by asking the children:
- What can you remember about the minibeasts you found?
- Where did you find them?
- What type of habitat did they prefer?

Resources
- Collecting vessels: small buckets, bags or baskets
- Straight sticks (approximately 60 cm in length)
- Collected natural materials: leaves, dead plant material, pine cones, and so on.

Main activity
Challenge the children to find some straight sticks. They will need to use their maths skills for this as the sticks need to be roughly the same length (60 cm). You might want to show them an example, as well as providing rulers or tape measures to assist with this and extend the learning. You will need enough sticks for groups of children to create their own small circle. The groups need to find areas of soft ground to push their sticks into vertically to make their circle. You can form one large circle instead.

Once constructed, the circles need to be filled with natural resources to create minibeast habitats. Give each child a collecting vessel and ask them to gather natural resources to fill their circle.

Extension ideas
- Develop the minibeast homes by making more circles and connecting them. Perhaps each addition could have a different function, just like the rooms of the children's homes.
- Monitor the habitats over a few weeks, inspecting them using magnifying glasses to see if there are any residents.
- Make a minibeast hotel by stacking wooden pallets and filling them with a variety of materials, such as stones, bamboo, straw, grass, mud, bricks, plants and twigs, to make lots of different habitats. Examples can be found online.

Reflections
On a dry day, ask the children to lie on the ground of your outdoor area and cover them with leaves and twigs, leaving their faces clear! Ask them to look up at the trees or sky and imagine what it would be like to be a minibeast crawling on the ground. The children can share how the experience felt, using descriptive language to inform the group.

Links to EYFS
- Physical development: Moving and handling (ELG 04)
- Understanding the world: The world (ELG 14).

Caterpillar art

You may discover caterpillars under leaves or eating the plants in your outdoor space in spring and summer! Collect some of these fascinating creatures carefully and watch how they grow and develop. Do not forget to provide them with some of the leaves they were found on, topping them up regularly.

Starter
Play Caterpillars and Butterflies. Ask the children to crawl around the site like caterpillars, either standing or lying on their front as they prefer. When you shout 'Butterflies', they must fly gracefully around the site using their new wings! You could give out coloured silks or scarves to act as wings.

Resources
• Mud
• Squares of white cotton
• Collected materials – items that will release colour when crushed. Be aware of what plants/berries are safe to use.
• Rubber mallets.

Main activity
Read the children *The Very Hungry Caterpillar* by Eric Carle, building an outdoor session on the story. If you have a mud kitchen, you could add some of the food from the story to it, or make your own out of mud. You could also make mud caterpillars, hiding them around the site for the children to find. Discuss where these creatures might like to live.

Have a go at creating symmetrical butterfly prints using gathered materials. To do so, take a small square of white cotton (an old bed sheet cut into pieces works well) and lay any collected materials on one half of the sheet. Fold the other half of the sheet over the decorated half. Hold it down and hit it all over with a rubber mallet. You should see the colours of the gathered items mixing together and colouring the top sheet. Open it and you will see a symmetrical butterfly. You could add a few details, such as legs and antennae with a black pen.

Extension ideas
• Make a tasty stew. Mix water, mud and anything the children gather to make a stew for the minibeasts in a big pan. Do not add any real creatures and emphasise that the stew is not to be eaten.

• Make a butterfly feeding station. Mash up some very ripe bananas, put the pulp on a paper plate and suspend it from a tree. Watch carefully to see if you have any visitors over the next few days.

Reflections
Butterflies have superpowers. One of these being that they can fly! Ask each child what one superpower they would choose for themselves. Would they, for example, fly like a butterfly, transform like a caterpillar, jump like a grasshopper or burrow like a worm?

Links to EYFS
• Understanding the world: The world (ELG 14)
• Expressive arts and design: Exploring and using media and materials (ELG 16)
• Expressive arts and design: Being imaginative (ELG 17).

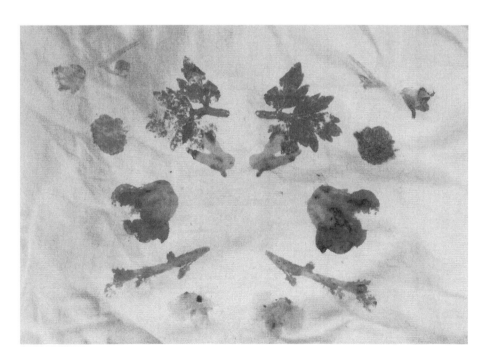

Busy as bees

Bees are extremely important creatures. They pollinate flowers, trees and crops, helping, in the process, to provide food for us. Children can be scared of bees because of their ability to sting. You may need to reassure them that bees only sting when under threat, so if the children are respectful, they should be fine.

Starter

Talk about bees with the children. Look at some pictures of bees and honeycomb, asking the children what they can tell you about them. Explain why bees are important and what roles they perform in nature.

Play a game during which the children are bees and must move their tiny wings very fast in order to fly around in a circle, all in one direction. Explain that when you clap your hands once, the wind changes direction and the bees must turn and go the other way around the circle. When you clap twice, the wind drops and the bees must sit until you tell them to resume their flight. Encourage lots of loud buzzing!

Resources

- Yellow wool
- Alder cones
- Bamboo
- Gloves
- Hacksaws
- Paper plates
- Blue, yellow and violet film
- Double-sided tape
- Scissors.

Main activity

Here are three bee ideas for you to try.

- Make bees by wrapping lengths of yellow wool around alder cones. Hang them from trees to make your own swarm!
- Cut bamboo into 15cm lengths using hacksaws. Children will need to wear gloves and be closely supervised. Tie the bamboo lengths together in bundles to make bee-nesting boxes. Hang these from trees and observe them over time to see if any bees move in. This type of habitat is suitable for solitary bees to nest in over winter.

- Make bee glasses. Bees see mostly in blues, yellows and violets. Cut out the centre of a paper plate, leaving the rim intact. Attach pieces of coloured film to this using double-sided tape, creating a bee lens through which to view the world. The children can decorate their lenses using gathered materials from your site to create exciting, personalised versions.

Extension ideas

- Play Bee Hide-and-Seek. Hide coloured pieces of card around your site and challenge the children to find one specific colour each. As they do so, they can pretend to be bees looking for brightly-coloured flowers.

Reflections

While bees are frightening for some children, others may find different things scary. Ask the children to find someone else in the group to talk to about what they find frightening. They need to take turns so both children are heard.

It is important to give children the opportunity to talk about what worries them and work through it, rather than glossing over it.

Give this activity time, and be prepared to join in with some of the discussions to reassure the children.

Links to EYFS

- Understanding the world: The world (ELG 14).

Webs and weaving

Spiders are fascinating creatures with lots of remarkable characteristics. Share some of the following facts with your children and ask if they know any others.
- Spiders are arachnids, not insects.
- Spiders have eight legs, while insects have six.
- Spiders do not have antennae, while insects do.
- Most spiders make silk, which they use to create a web to capture prey.
- Abandoned spiders' webs are called cobwebs.

Starter

Explore your setting with the children to see if you can find any spiders. Good places to look are in trees, between tall plant stems and in gaps in stone or brick walls. On a cold morning when there is dew in the air, spiders' webs will catch droplets and sparkle in the light, shimmering like beautiful jewels. Carefully collect and examine any spiders you find, observing their body parts and legs. Take photographs of them to use for an indoor display. Remember to return the spiders to a spot near where they were found.

Resources

- Rope
- String
- Forked sticks
- Wool.

Main activity

To encourage physical play provide ropes and string, challenging the children to make their own spider's web in a tree or bush. This could be done all together or in several smaller groups. Children might wrap and tie rope around a tree or bush, trying to cover as much of it as possible, leaving only small gaps. Once they have done this, they could attach objects, such as feathers, sticks, leaves and twigs, to represent the flies the spider has caught.

On a smaller scale, give out forked sticks for the children to wrap wool around, making mini-spiders' webs, which they can take home with them.

Extension ideas

- Allow children to use rope to help each other out of a pit of mud, or to pull each other gently around the outdoor space. In each case, explain that the rope represents spiders' silk.
- Lay a small tyre on the ground and fill the centre with fine sand or flour. Show the children how to draw a spider's web design in the surface, before wiping it clean and inviting them to have a go. This is an ideal way to practise fine motor skills.

Reflections

Standing in a circle, give the end of a ball of string to a child who would like to say something about the session. When they have finished, you give the ball to the next child who would like to speak, while the first child keeps hold of the end of the string. This second child speaks and holds on to part of the length of string. This continues until all have spoken or passed if they do not wish to speak. Explain that the resultant string pattern represents the connections in a spider's web, and how we are also all connected as people.

Links to EYFS

- Mathematics: Shape, space and measures (ELG 12)
- Understanding the world: The world (ELG 14).

Wormery watching

Worms are a very important part of any ecosystem, helping to break down organic matter and enrich the soil. Encourage an appreciation of these misunderstood creatures by using the activities below.

Starter

Ask the children to share what they know about worms. Show pictures of worms and talk about their environmental impact: producing compost, aerating soil and eating decomposing matter. Dig a hole to see if you can find some worms. The best places to do this are damp shady areas or newly-disturbed soil. Be careful not to harm the worms.

Other ways of collecting worms include:
• Lay a damp piece of cardboard over some newly-dug soil or grass. Carefully lift the cardboard in the evening or early in the morning. While worms cannot hear, they can sense vibrations, so tread lightly!
• Drive a small stake into the ground and then tap or vibrate it. The worms will mistake the vibrations for a mole digging nearby and come to the surface to avoid it.

The best way to view worms is in a tray filled with damp soil. Worms breathe through their skin, so this minimises the amount of handling.

Resources

• Magnifying glasses
• Large jar with lid
• Gravel, sand and soil
• Leaves and grass
• Water.

Main activity

Once you have collected your worms, give the children magnifying glasses to examine them in detail. Can they spot the different body parts: head, mouth, saddle and tail? You could photograph a worm, labelling the parts when indoors.

Create a simple wormery. Add a layer of gravel to a large glass or plastic jar. This will help with drainage. Add layers of sand and soil until the jar is almost full, leaving room for a layer of fresh leaves and grass. Add a small amount of water to keep the worms moist, and then add the worms. Punch some holes in the lid to aid airflow and attach it to the jar. Keep the jar in a dark place. Over time, the worms will pull the leaves and grass into their burrows, mixing the sand and soil as they dig. Make sure the wormery stays moist and monitor it over time with the children. Add food as necessary.

Extension ideas

• Use charcoal or a pencil to draw the worms you find.
• Make worms from mud or clay, commenting on their body parts.
• Make a larger wormery using bought compost or creating your own. Add some worms, topping the heap up regularly with vegetable peelings and fruit. Monitor for any changes.
• Dig holes, creating mini-habitats for worms. Children can use their imagination to design a super wormery, including rooms, swimming pools, parks or play spaces!

Reflections

Give the children magnifying glasses and ask them to crawl on their front like worms to learn how it might feel to be one. Can they describe what they see and feel? What are the similarities and differences between humans and worms?

Links to EYFS

• Understanding the world: The world (ELG 14).

Even with a small site, you may be surprised by the traces of animal activity you find. Get to know your outdoor space throughout the seasons to benefit fully from it, and to make it a safe haven for wildlife.

Starter

Look round your site for signs that animals have visited. Use your findings to create an animal scavenger hunt for the children. This may include feathers, fleece or fur hanging from fences, worm holes, animal tracks, and so on. Print photographs of these signs, laminating them so they can be used outdoors repeatedly. Children can be very literal, so only print things they are likely to find!

If a limited range of wildlife visits your site, research how you could encourage more visitors. The activities below will help.

Resources

• Twigs and branches
• Big bucket
• Stones
• Bird boxes.

Main activity

To make your outdoor area more attractive to wildlife, let it go wild! Talk with the children about the importance of creating safe spaces for animals, and then try the following.
• Make a habitat pile. Ask the children to pile twigs, branches and leaves into a heap, which must then be left. This will be a valuable home for hedgehogs and other small mammals, as well as minibeasts.
• Make a mini-pond. Use an old sink or big bucket with large stones in the bottom. Fill it with water from an existing pond. There will be lots of life in the water already, so all you need to do is watch it develop! Make sure you leave some stones close to the edge so frogs and other amphibians can climb in and out.
• Let the grass grow. Section off an area of grass and monitor it over a few weeks to see what happens. You will find that lots of species of flowering plants are probably already present, which, in turn, will attract bees and other pollinators to your garden.
• Put up bird boxes. This is an adult activity, but involve the children in choosing where to place the boxes and watching them to see when residents move in. Provide a quiet place to observe from, and use identification sheets, so the children can start to learn which birds are visiting.

Extension ideas

• Keep a note of animals that visit your wildlife garden. Take photographs or draw pictures to record them.
• Put out bird feeders near a window so the children can watch the birds from indoors.
• Ask the children what their gardens are like. They may want to bring pictures in to share. You may get some more ideas for your outdoor area too.

Reflections

Quietly sitting and watching birds or staring at your reflection in a pond are good calming activities. You could provide comfortable cushions and blankets near the wildlife area. Ask the children to imagine what it would be like to be a bird or to live in an underwater world.

Links to EYFS

• Physical development: Moving and handling (ELG 04)
• Understanding the world: The world (ELG 14).

Growing seeds

Simple growing activities are a great way to engage children with the outdoors, teach them where food comes from and encourage healthy eating habits. Start with the basics, and be prepared to get your hands dirty!

Starter

Talk with the children about where different foods they eat come from. Ask if anyone can tell you how a bean grows. It may help to show them some broad bean seeds as some of the children might not have handled seeds before.

Soak a broad bean seed in water overnight and show the children how you can peel the outer casing off and split the bean in half. Having done this, you will be able to see the tiny leaf and root beginning to form. Ask older children if they can recognise the parts of a plant and suggest what their function might be.

Resources

- Bean seeds
- Cardboard tubes
- Newspaper
- Small empty fruit trays (strawberry trays work well)
- Compost
- Wooden lolly sticks
- Pens
- Watering can.

Main activity

Once you have discussed the purpose of growing seeds, explain that the children are going to make some pots and plant bean seeds to see if the plants will grow strong and tall. Take a cardboard tube and a small sheet of newspaper. Roll the newspaper around the tube, leaving a small bit of tube showing. Tuck one end of the newspaper in and remove the tube. You now have a newspaper pot ready for use! Once you have demonstrated this, the children can make more, putting them into plastic fruit trays to keep them upright.

When you have enough pots, fill them nearly to the top with compost. Tap each pot to settle the soil and then make a hole in it with your finger or a pen that matches the length of a bean seed. Pop a bean seed in and cover it with compost. Do not forget to label the pots using a wooden lolly stick (minimising plastic waste) with the date and type of seed planted. Water the compost and place the trays in a light spot outdoors or on a windowsill if it is still cold. Remember, the back of the seed packet will have further information.

Extension ideas

- Ask the children to use natural materials to create pictures of what they think the seeds will grow into.
- Check the seeds on a daily basis and water as necessary.
- Measure the plants as they grow and record your findings using standard or non-standard measurements.
- Take photographs at every stage and make a diary of the seed's growth.
- Try planting different seeds, such as cress, salad crops, radishes or carrots. All of these can be harvested and eaten raw.

Reflections

Ask the children if they can think of anything else that grows from small to big. They may well suggest themselves. Ask if they can think of something they could not do when they were younger, but can do now. Invite them to tell a friend what it is. How does this make them feel? How about thinking of something they will be able to do when they are even older.

Links to EYFS

- Mathematics: Shape, space and measures (ELG 12)
- Understanding the world: The world (ELG 14).

Den designers

 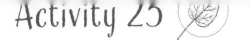

> Making large dens can be difficult for young children, whose strength and coordination are still maturing. Better to start small and work towards bigger challenges. You might need to assist with moving some materials and basic construction, but make sure the ideas come from the children.

Starter

Discuss the idea of place and why homes are important to people. Ask the children what they would have in their perfect home if they could have anything. Use these ideas to build up a picture of what might be included in a den. You could use a piece of flipchart paper to record the ideas.

Play Hide and Seek to help the children start thinking about good places to build a secret den. Encourage the children to stay still in their hiding places, giving them time to feel what it is like to be there. As the seeker, only point to a child if they move, even if you see them when still.

Resources

- Sheets
- Coloured silks or material
- Pegs or similar clips
- String
- Bamboo poles
- Small branches
- Toy woodland animals
- Nets
- Tarpaulins
- Small-world figures
- Log slices
- Pine cones
- Sticks
- Stones
- Biodegradable glitter.

Main activity

There are lots of ways of including construction and den building in your outdoor sessions, both adult-led activities and self-directed investigations. Remember that the aim is to encourage the children to be independent learners. You may need to support their learning, but step back when you can.

Here are some of our favourite ways to encourage den building:
- After reading a story about animal homes, use natural materials to create mini-dens for animals. Use toy woodland animals to bring the dens to life.
- Create easy-to-construct lean-tos using sheets, pegs/clips and poles.
- Collect branches and leaves from a local park or ask for donations from parents/carers to make natural shelters.
- Make a basic tepee from bamboo poles tied together with string. Allow the children to decorate it with ribbon, coloured fabric, large silks and netting.
- Provide small tarpaulins, ropes and clips to make a den from the lower branches of a tree or bush.
- Make dens for small-world figures using stones, log slices, twigs, feathers and pine cones. Add some biodegradable glitter for extra sparkle.

Extension ideas
- Challenge the children to make a den using natural materials alone.
- Work together to make a shelter you can all gather under. You might need to build the main structure beforehand, allowing the children to add layers of shelter and decoration.
- Provide household items for imaginary den play: pots, pans, cushions, sheets, curtains, and so on.

Reflections

Sitting in a den they have created is a great place for children to reflect on and talk about the building experience. Invite them to sit in the den and use pencils and paper to draw how they feel. When finished, they can share their picture with a friend should they wish.

Links to EYFS
- Physical development: Moving and handling (ELG 04).

Children learn a lot about themselves through self-directed play in the outdoors. To complement this, we can offer activities and experiences designed to develop identity and self-awareness.

Starter
Prepare pictures of different facial expressions, printing and laminating examples or painting them on log slices. Give each child a piece of card with their name on. Ask them to put it next to the picture that best represents how they are feeling. Invite them to tell a friend why they are feeling like this and whether they enjoy this feeling or not. Allow time for reflection and offer each child the opportunity to tell the group how they are feeling.

Resources
• Examples of self-portraits or portraits
• Natural materials.

Main activity
Look at some examples of self-portraits with the group, discussing how the artists have used portraiture to represent their face or that of another. What do they think of the artwork you have shown them?

Challenge the children to collect natural materials individually or in pairs from your outdoor space to make their own self-portraits. Show the children how they can make a picture frame on the ground from sticks in which to create their portrait. Encourage them to think about the colours and shapes they are using.

For a harder challenge, ask a child to lie down while you create an outline of their body with leaves or sticks. When they get up, they can fill in the outlined space with natural materials to make it colourful. Challenge the children to add key features and details: a face, fingers, toes and, even, clothes.

Extension ideas
• Use natural materials to create faces indoors.
• Use a paper plate as a base for a self-portrait, adding laminated labels to indicate the features.

• Look at different styles of portraiture, such as impressionistic or abstract, challenging the children to recreate them using natural materials.
• Draw round a hand or foot on a piece of card and fill it with natural materials.
• Make clay or mud self-portraits.

Reflections
Ask the children to think of three reasons why it is good to be them. Invite them to tell a friend why they are happy as themselves. Perhaps they could suggest some reasons why their friend is unique too.

Links to EYFS
• Personal, social and emotional development: Managing feelings and behaviour (ELG 07).

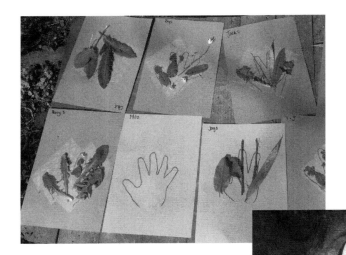

Our senses help us to interpret the world, and young children need opportunities to develop them and practise using them. The activities below help to engage children with the outdoors – an incredibly rich environment for sensory development. They also allow space to acknowledge the challenges that those with sensory difficulties face in their daily lives.

Starter

Mark out five areas of your outdoor space, each related to a different sense. You can use relevant pictures to indicate the different zones. Take an object from your setting and mime exploring it with one of your senses: smell some fresh grass, listen to two sticks tapping together, look at a colourful flower, and so on. The children must work out which sense you are using and run to the related area. For younger children, you could just shout the sense.

Resources
• Leaf windows
• Small safety mirrors.

Main activity

Go on a nature walk around your site, asking the children to use four of their senses to explore the area.

Touch – Look for different textures: prickly, soft, hard, smooth. Discuss why materials feel different to each other and describe the sensations.

Sight – Use a leaf window: a piece of card with a square hole in it used to view leaves against the sky, examining the colours and shapes. Other activities include holding a mirror up to your nose horizontally and viewing the canopy above in it, or finding different colours that match your skin tone or clothes.

Hearing – Invite the children to sit and listen to the natural world and describe what they hear. Ask the children to name a sound they heard and think of a word to describe it. This will encourage a link between the sensory experience and the language used to describe it.

Smell – Go on a smell walk, investigating the smells you encounter. Ask the children to describe them, perhaps thinking of them in relation to the other senses. Are the smells loud, sharp, bright or smooth?

Extension ideas
• Capture the smell walk in photographs and use them to make a sensory display, recording electronically the words the children used.
• Build a session around each sense or challenge groups of children to explore the site using only one sense.
• For older children, give each child an adjective and ask them to look for a natural item that relates to their word. They can show the rest of the children what they have found, asking them to guess their adjective.

Reflections

Limiting the generally more dominant visual sense changes our perception of our surroundings. Give out blindfolds and encourage the children to find a quiet spot to sit, cover their eyes and experience the world without seeing it. Ask open questions to encourage a deeper understanding of place. What did you experience? How did it feel? How do you think animals use their senses to explore the world?

Links to EYFS
• Personal, social and emotional development: Managing feelings and behaviour (ELG 07).

Light and dark

> Some children are frightened of the dark and may be nervous of talking about it. However, given the opportunity, children can often come to terms with their fears and find a new confidence.

Starter

Read a story about the dark: *Owl Babies* by Martin Waddell and Patrick Benson is a good introduction. Ask the children:
• How do you think the owl babies felt in the dark without their mother?
• Have any of you ever felt like the owl babies?
• Would you like to tell us more?

Introduce some toy woodland animals and talk about their homes: foxes live in dens in the ground and owls live in hollow trees or barns. Print out pictures of each animal's home and see if the children can match the toy animal with their home. Ask the children which animals like to live in the daylight and which prefer the dark. Discuss why this might be the case.

The children could make homes for the toy animals, either dark, underground ones or light, airy versions.

Resources
• Card
• Double-sided tape
• White sheet
• Tealights
• Matches or safety lighter
• Clay.

Main activity

Still thinking about light and dark, ask the children to look for objects that match these criteria in your outdoor area. Use the gathered material to create two pictures: a light one and a dark one. Stick the relevant items onto a piece of card with double-sided tape, or arrange them on a white sheet. You may want to display the compositions side by side to emphasise the contrasts.

Talk with the children about sources of light. Can they think of ways to create light outdoors without access to electricity? Discuss fire and candles as sources of light, asking:
• What happens when a lighted candle is brought into a room?
• Where does the darkness go?

Light a candle and talk about the safety considerations involved in using fire.

Give out balls of clay and show the children how to push a tealight into one to make a simple candle holder. They can collect natural non-flammable materials to push into their holders as decoration.

Extension ideas
• Make dark dens for the children to hide in and explore.
• Use torches to explore dark places. Try covering the lens with coloured cellophane to change the light's colour.
• Use descriptive words to explain how it feels to be in the dark.
• Go outdoors when it is nearly dark during the winter.

Reflections

Sit underneath a big blanket or tarpaulin with a small group of children and ask them how it feels to be in the dark. Give each child an opportunity to think of a word that reflects their thoughts and something that would make them feel safe. You could link this back to *Owl Babies*.

Links to EYFS
• Mathematics: Shape, space and measures (ELG 12)
• Understanding the world: The world (ELG 14).

Find and describe

> The outdoor environment can be a fantastic stimulus for language and literacy. Children need to use their senses to help develop their literacy skills, and the outdoors is full of such opportunities.

Starter

Once you have gathered in your outdoor area, ask the children to close their eyes and focus on what they can hear, smell and feel. This helps to heighten these senses, which can be overshadowed by our dominant visual sense. You could extend this by making a 'feely bag' – a bag containing unusual natural objects of different shapes and textures. A child places their hand in the bag, feels one of the objects and describes it to the other children, helping them to guess what it is.

Resources

- Sticks
- iPad or sound recorder.

Main activity

Play It's Not a Stick. Ask the children to find a stick each and then regather. Challenge them to think of something that their stick could represent: a fishing rod or a magic wand, and so on. Now that the children have got the hang of describing objects as like something else (also called a metaphor), challenge them to try this with something that interests them from your outdoor area: an unusual leaf, a pretty stone, a colourful flower. Ask them to make up a story about what they imagine it is and how it got to be there. For example, an acorn cup could be a fairy's drinking vessel, while a green leaf might be a boat for a tribe of ants. Younger children may need some assistance, so have some adults available to offer help. Give children the opportunity to share their stories with the rest of the group. You could make audio recordings to play later.

Extension ideas

- Create a story using more than one object.
- Younger children may need some prompts:
  - 'Can you find a flower that looks like a dragon's hat?'
  - 'Can you discover a stick small enough to be a toothpick for a mouse?'
- Draw pictures of the stories either outdoors or inside.
- Use the children's items as objects in a feely bag.

Reflections

Ask the children to use their language skills to describe their feelings about the session. Use pictures of faces with different expressions that the children pick from to indicate how they feel about the session. Provide a range of emotions, remembering to allow for negative, as well as positive responses.

Links to EYFS

- Physical development: Moving and handling (ELG 04)
- Understanding the world: The world (ELG 14).

© In all Weathers! – Yellow DoorPermission to Photocopy 34

Use your outside space and what it holds to practise letter sounds and names by looking for natural or manufactured objects whose initial letters can be used to create an outdoor A–Z.

Starter

Go for a group welly wander around your site looking for interesting natural and manufactured objects. When someone spots an item, ask them if they can work out as a group what the first letter and/or sound is.

Repeat the activity with the children looking for items that begin with the same sound as their own name or that of another group member. If you cannot collect the items, take photographs of them.

Resources
• Alphabet stones or log slices
• Camera
• Collected items (see above).

Main activity

You will need a set of 26 stones or log slices, each painted with a different letter of the alphabet. You can buy these or create your own. Lay the letters out in alphabetical order and talk about the letter sounds with the children. Can anyone find the letter that their name starts with? After this, you will need the collected objects from the starter activity or laminated copies of the photographs you took during a previous session. Can the children match the objects with the letter sounds, creating an outdoors alphabet? This can make a lovely display/resource if each item is photographed and printed out along with its letter.

Extension ideas
• Practise letter formation by drawing with sticks in mud or sand.
• For older children, give out paper plates and allow them to make their own letters using natural materials.
• Give children specific sounds and challenge them to find matching sounds in nature.
• Use numbers as well as letters. For example, can they find three pine cones or eight leaves?

Reflections

Stand in a circle without any gaps. Throw a soft ball from one child to another, with each recipient given an opportunity to share the sound their name starts with and an animal/tree/flower that also starts with that sound. Make sure everyone has the chance to speak should they want to.

Links to EYFS
• Literacy: Reading (ELG 09)
• Literacy: Writing (ELG 10).

Nature's maths

Numeracy skills can be approached in many different ways outdoors. Often it is through repetition or play that children begin to really understand mathematical concepts.

Starter

Go on a maths hunt in your outdoor area. Try a scavenger version during which the children try to find specific items, such as the following:
- A square
- Something with three sides
- An object larger than a car
- Something with curved edges
- A leaf with five sections
- Something with a straight line marked on it
- A sphere
- Something heavier than you.

Resources
- Sticks
- Leaves
- Collecting trays
- Laminated numbers
- Wooden spoons
- Measuring sticks
- Rope
- Mirrors.

Main activity

Here are some of our favourite ways to encourage children's mathematical thinking outdoors:
- Ask the children to stand in a circle. Shout the name of a shape, which the children then need to make using their bodies. This might be standing up or lying on the ground, depending on each child's inclination.
- Make shapes using natural objects, for example, a square using sticks or a circle using leaves.
- Give out trays, each with a laminated number in. Challenge the children to find that number of objects or an item with that many sides.

- Use wooden spoons with numbers on to collect really small items.
- Cut sticks to a specific length and use them to measure the distance from one place to another in your outdoor area.
- Make a number line with rope and labels, asking the children to collect the right number of objects for each label.
- Use mirrors to investigate reflective symmetry.

Extension ideas
- Link these activities to indoor themes.
- Take a picture of the number line and display it in your setting.
- Use mathematical language while carrying out other activities:
  – Is the stick straight or curved?
  – How many leaves can we count?
  – What shapes can you see outside?

Reflections

Continue the theme by asking the children to line up in order of height. Are they taller or shorter than their friends? Once they are in order, ask each child to share something they have learned during the session. It is also useful to ask them what they have not understood so you know what to focus on next time.

Links to EYFS
- Mathematics: Numbers (ELG 11)
- Mathematics: Shape, space and measures (ELG 12).

Natural colours

 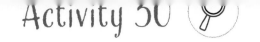

Looking at colours in the natural world can stimulate both children's visual sense and their curiosity. Try the activities below throughout the year to explore any differences, and why they may have taken place.

Starter

Talk with the children about the colours they may find outdoors. Depending on when you are doing this activity, you might want to draw the children's attention to the bright, vivid greens of spring or the dull browns and greys of winter.

Give the children colour match cards made from paint samples to help focus their attention on some of the naturally occurring colours in your outdoor area. Match the colours you give the children to the time of year. Ask them to bring their coloured items back to your gathering place for discussion.

At the end of the activity, give the children a chance to talk about the colours they found and where they discovered them.

Resources

- Reusable plastic cups
- Strong spoons
- Gloves
- Sticks
- Water
- Paintbrushes
- Squares of white material
- Paper
- Resources for natural paint (see below).

Main activity

Once the children have explored the colours they discovered, discuss how they might use them. Hopefully someone will mention painting! Explain that you are going to make natural paint together using resources from the outdoor environment. You can mention that this is how people made paint and dyes in the past.

Give each child a strong spoon to collect the item they want to use to create their paint, and a reusable plastic cup to hold it. The following materials produce good clear colours.

- Mud
- Charcoal
- Chalk (different colours)
- Blackberries or wild raspberries
- Nettles (soaked and squeezed hard to release their juice – a job for an adult)
- Spices, such as turmeric
- Flowers: only pick if they are non-toxic and very common.

Provide gloves for gathering fruit or berries from spiky bushes.

Once the children have collected their chosen base, they add some water to it, squashing and stirring the mixture to produce paint. This can then be painted onto squares of white material (an old cut up bed sheet works well) or paper.

Extension ideas

- Add aromatics (essential oils are good) and other materials, such as biodegradable glitter, to your paints.
- Paint on a big sheet as a group, with each child adding to the picture.
- Paint on other natural objects, such as stones, log slices or trees.
- Make face paints using natural non-toxic ingredients. Do not use goosegrass as it can produce a rash.

Reflections

The children can use their paints on a paper plate to create a face representing how they feel about the session. It is important that we allow children to express a whole range of emotions and do not always assume they have enjoyed an activity. Giving them space to discuss emotions can be a valuable learning opportunity.

Links to EYFS

- Understanding the world: The world (ELG 14)
- Expressive arts and design: Exploring and using media and materials (ELG 16)
- Expressive arts and design: Being imaginative (ELG 17).

Messy painting

Extend the creative opportunities you offer to your children by taking your art curriculum outdoors and working on a large scale. By doing physical art, children are using their whole bodies, practising gross motor skills and developing their creativity.

Starter

Art and other creative activities often involve looking at colours, so spend some time talking about the natural colours in your outdoor area. Go on a colour hunt, encouraging the children to look for specific colours, such as green, brown or yellow. Alternatively, use more generic words, such as 'light' and 'dark'.

This use of language will help develop children's vocabulary, giving them the words they need to explore the world around them.

Resources

• Tarpaulin
• Plank of wood
• Roll of wallpaper
• Powder paint
• Poster paint
• Water (or rain!)
• Pots and spoons.

Main activity

To continue your exploration of colour, set up a tarpaulin at an angle or attach a length of wallpaper to a sloping plank of wood. Put different colours of powder paint in pots and give the children spoons. Invite them to put spoonfuls of paint on the highest edge of the tarpaulin or paper. Once they have done this, tip water onto the paint from above, or let the rain do the work, washing the colours down the slope, mixing and blending as they go. Explore such questions as:
• What has happened to the colours as they have run down the tarpaulin/wallpaper?
• What might happen if we mix two colours together?
• What are the names of these new colours?

Try this activity with poster paint to see how the colours move.

If you can get hold of a sheet of clear Perspex®, run the colours down it as described above, allowing the children to sit underneath the sheet and watch the movement of the paint. Use the opportunity to discuss what is happening and why, making sure you ask plenty of questions to extend the children's learning.

Extension ideas

• Make handprints of different colours on paper or log slices.
• Paint on old bed sheets hung from trees – these are less likely to go soggy in the rain.
• Draw on kitchen paper with washable felt-tipped pens. Leave the pictures out in the rain and watch the colours bleed and blend.

Reflections

Colours can be used to represent feelings and emotions, so you could ask the children the following:
• What colour would you be if you had to choose?
• What colour did you feel like when you woke up this morning?
• What about last night?

Using such questions gives children the chance to express their feelings using visual imagery. It also allows them to reflect on how their feelings change during the course of a day. This all helps to develop their emotional literacy.

Links to EYFS

• Expressive arts and design: Exploring and using media and materials (ELG 16)
• Expressive arts and design: Being imaginative (ELG 17).

Outdoor art

Children love to use their whole bodies to create large-scale artwork, which provides a great opportunity for developing gross motor skills. Supplying children with lots of resources to be creative ensures that all are included and have a chance to express their ideas.

Starter

As this can be a very physical activity, start on a small scale to get the children thinking about what it means to be creative. Look at some artwork by land artists such as Andy Goldsworthy and James Brunt. Ask the children what they think of it and discuss any ideas it prompts.

Gather some natural materials beforehand in readiness for this activity, and top up the selection with the children once outside. It is useful to have quite a lot of resources, so a bit of preparation will make a big difference to the success of the activity. Stones, sticks, feathers, shells, leaves and pine cones all work well.

Give each child a white piece of cloth or a paper plate on which to arrange some of the natural objects into a pattern or picture. Talk to the children about what they are creating and give them an opportunity to share their work if they want to.

Resources
• Natural materials
• White sheet
• Mops
• Brooms
• Brushes
• Buckets
• Spray bottles
• Sponges
• Water
• Materials to paint with: commercial paint, mud, and non-toxic berries / leaves / flowers mixed with water.

Main activity

To create large-scale artwork, you need a big canvas! This may be a wall, fence or large sheet suspended between two trees. Make your own colours using the materials above, applying it with the tools listed. Being outdoors means you do not need to worry about the mess, so go for it!

You can encourage the children to paint on other objects, such as logs, branches and trees. This will not harm the trees.

Extension ideas
• Make a big picture frame out of sticks laid on the ground and invite the children to put natural objects within it to make a communal piece of artwork.
• Use collected items as paintbrushes. Try sticks or feathers.
• Splatter the paint with lots of water for a different effect.

Reflections

Art is subjective, so ask the children how they feel about what they have created. Do they think it is more important that people like it or that they had fun making it? What is the reason for creating art in the first place? Can the children find a friend whose art they like and tell them why? Give feedback to all the children on what you like about their creations.

Links to EYFS
• Understanding the world: The world (ELG 14).
• Expressive arts and design: Exploring and using media and materials (ELG 16)
• Expressive arts and design: Being imaginative (ELG 17).

Magic potions

This activity is ideal for Halloween, when spells and potions are on children's minds. It is good for exploring an outdoor area and making collections, providing an opportunity to practise sorting and counting. You will need to do a little preparation: writing a spell and gathering some resources. It is well worth the effort!

Starter

Beforehand, screw up a piece of paper, flatten it and soak it in cold tea to dye it. Once dry, write a spell on it. The spell needs to include ingredients that can be found in your outdoor area, along with some words for the children to repeat as a chant to make the magic happen. Use easily identifiable items, such as stones, sticks, pine cones, leaves, and so on. Finally, hide the spell somewhere in your site.

Prepare your cauldron by placing some 'treasure' in it and covering it with some coloured material.

Explain that there is an ancient spell hidden in the outdoor area and you need the children's help to find it. Send them off to look for it. With a big group, you may want to have more than one spell, splitting the children into smaller groups.

Resources

- Prepared magic spell
- Big cauldron or pan
- Piece of coloured material
- Some 'treasure': edible varieties work well!
- Wooden spoon or stick.

Main activity

Once the spell has been found, read the list of ingredients aloud, asking the children what they think will happen once the spell is cast. Be prepared for some very imaginative answers!

As you read the list aloud a second time, ask the children to help you by collecting the required items. Add these to the cauldron and stir the mixture with a wooden spoon or stick, saying the words of the spell and doing some magical gesturing! After some theatrics,

take out whatever treasure you hid under the material and show it to the children. You could use anything for the treasure. Use your imagination!

Extension ideas

- Give out reusable plastic cups and challenge the children to create their own magic potions using water, food colouring, biodegradable glitter and resources from nearby. Emphasise that these potions are not to be drunk!
- Challenge each child to think of a name for their potion and decide what effect it will have.

Use this activity as a starting point for potion making in a mud kitchen or messy-play area.

Reflections

Allow the children time to share their potions, asking them to talk about how they smell, what they look like and what effects they might have. Encourage the use of descriptive language.

Discuss with the children how they felt about the activity. End by asking, 'If you could cast any magic spell, what would it be, and why?'

Links to EYFS

- Physical development: Moving and handling (ELG 04)
- Understanding the world: The world (ELG 14).

Woodland fairies

This play activity uses familiar mythical creatures to spark children's interest in the outdoors. Talk with the group about some of the fantastical creatures they are aware of from stories: fairies, goblins and pixies might come up.
• What do you think they look like?
• Where do they live?
• What do they like to do?

Starter
Before the session, sprinkle some biodegradable glitter in several places around your outdoor area. Make it look like something has landed there briefly, dropping some glitter as it flew away.

Tell the children you have spotted some evidence of activity in the area, asking them if they can help you to investigate what it is. Show them some of the glitter, asking them why it has appeared. Be careful to ask open questions. The children will come up with their own ideas as to what has left these magical marks. Once you have shared ideas, allow the children to look for more of the marks. Give them plenty of time to explore and use their imagination.

Resources
• Pictures of fairy houses from books, the Internet or drawn from your imagination
• Fairy doors (wooden decorated doors: purchased or home-made)
• Traditional wooden pegs
• Felt tip pens
• Coloured wool or string
• Coloured feathers
• Clay
• Matchsticks
• Acorn cups
• Blocks of wood for making furniture
• Corks (whole and halved).

Main activity
Show the pictures of the fairy houses to the children, explaining that they are going to make some for the fairies in your setting. What would the houses need to include to keep the fairies safe and comfortable? Ideas may include:
• Roof
• Front door
• Kitchen
• Bathroom
• Table and chairs
• Food
• Decoration.

Invite the children to make their own fairy houses. The items listed in Resources are useful for this activity. Feel free to make suggestions, but do not forget to allow plenty of opportunities for experimentation.

Extension ideas
• Make clay models of the fairies who live in the houses.
• Make mini-furniture using clay and matchsticks.
• Use old-fashioned wooden pegs to make fairies, decorating them using pens and natural materials.
• Make up stories about the fairies and the adventures they have when no-one else is nearby.

Reflections
Whenever the children make something during a session, it is important to let them talk about it if they want to. Leave time at the end of this session to visit all of the homes, inviting the children to tell the rest of the group what they have done.

You could use a fairy puppet or figure as an aid to the children's reflections. Use it to ask the children open-ended questions about their experiences during the activity.

Links to EYFS
• Personal, social and emotional development: Making relationships (ELG 08).

Dragon footsteps

> Dragons, as with other mythical creatures, can really spark children's imagination and lead to lots of self-directed creative play. However, introduce such imaginary creatures with caution as some children might be a little scared at first.

Starter

Play Follow the Dragon on the way to your outdoor area, with an adult as the head of the dragon and the children following as the body and tail. The rest of the dragon must copy whatever movement or action the leader makes as they wind their way to your gathering place. Try running on tiptoes, jumping a deep river or crawling on all fours!

Resources

• A dragon story
• Blindfold
• Treasure: metal bell or jewellery.

Main activity

Talk with the children about what they know about dragons. Ask questions and prompts to carry out a 'knowledge harvest'.
• Where do you think dragons come from?
• Where might they live?
• Who would like to tell a story that includes a dragon?

Share a story with a dragon in it, or make one up with the children.

After this introduction, play Sleeping Dragons. Form a circle and ask one child to sit in the middle, blindfolded and with some treasure beside them. Choose a child to sneak in from the circle's edge and try to steal the treasure. If the dragon hears their approach, they point to where they think the sound is coming from. If they are correct, it is someone else's turn to be the dragon. If not, the game continues. This is a great game to encourage children to listen and be as quiet as possible.

Extension ideas

• Make homes for dragons out of materials from your outdoor area, natural or introduced, imagining where they might like to live and what they might need to keep them safe.
• Hide plastic toy dragons in a sand or mud pit for the children to find and dig up.

• Make dragons' eggs out of mud, allowing them to harden before painting them to create magical dragons' eggs.

Reflections

Pass a toy dragon around the circle, giving each child a chance to tell it what they have enjoyed or found challenging about the session.

Links to EYFS

• Personal, social and emotional development: Making relationships (ELG 08).

Pirate fun

Whenever you can, base your activity plans and ideas on the children's interests and previous experiences. This gives a sense of continuity and builds on existing passions to really engage the children with their learning. Pirates are a perennial favourite of many young children and provide rich outdoor learning opportunities.

Starter

This may be a topic that you are already covering indoors. If so, the children will know a lot about pirates already. To introduce this topic outdoors, tell a pirate story, acting out the key events with the children. Alternatively, go on a pirate scavenger hunt. Can the children find natural objects that look like the following items?
• Pirate's eye patch
• Treasure map
• Wooden leg
• Pirate treasure
• Pirate ship
• Some sand from the beach.

You can create your own printed scavenger list with text and/or pictures.

Resources
• Sticks
• Logs.

Main activity

Explain to the children that they are going to build a pirate boat for an epic voyage. To do this, ask each child to find a stick and bring it to a chosen area with enough room to make a group circle. When you have formed a circle, make the outline of a pirate ship's hull. It helps if one child stands at the front (bow) of the ship, one at the back (stern) and the others make the sides (port and starboard). Once you have a rough shape, place the sticks on the ground to complete the outline. You can always adjust the sticks once they are laid down. Ask the children to find more sticks to build up the sides of the ship, create masts, sails, a plank, a ship's wheel, and so on.

Extension ideas
• The children can create their own scavenger lists of other things pirates might need.
• Make a treasure map of your site, marking on it where some treasure has been hidden, and challenging the children to find it.
• Hide pirate treasure in your sand or mud area.
• Make pirate flags out of old white pillowcases. The children can decorate them with mud or paint made from charcoal.

Reflections

Lay a piece of rope on the ground and ask each child to stand along its length at a point that corresponds with how much they have enjoyed the session. To simplify this, place two hoops on the floor, one for 'good'; the other for 'not good'. Ask the children to stand in the hoop that represents how they feel.

Links to EYFS
• Personal, social and emotional development: Making relationships (ELG 08).

Teddy bears' picnic

A teddy bears' picnic always captures young children's attention and is a great activity for a sunny day outdoors. Invite the children to bring in an old teddy from home for the picnic. You may want to extend the invitation to parents/carers so they can join in the fun and keep an eye on the bears!

Starter

Set up your outdoor area with a blanket on the ground, paper plates, cups and, of course, teddy bears! When the children come out, explain to them that, although the picnic is nearly ready, there is no food yet. Ask them to help by collecting some natural materials to finish getting the feast ready for the bears. Perhaps they could collect sticks to represent fish fingers, stones as peas, mud as soup, acorns as pasta. Let their imagination lead.

Resources

- Water
- Mud
- Chalk
- Collected materials
- Pots, pans, spoons, and so on.

Main activity

Once the food has been collected, the feast can begin! Provide pots, pans and spoons or use the resources in your mud kitchen to mix the ingredients with water and mud. Serve up the mixtures for the bears to enjoy.

Allow the children to decorate any trees around the picnic area with mud or chalk, making the area more exciting for the bears. They can build seats for the bears using logs and other collected items. They can even build the bears homes or shelters using sticks and leaves to keep them cool during the hot weather.

This activity is a great opportunity to develop the children's natural creativity and imagination, so try not to intervene and allow them to explore. Sometimes all we need to do is stand back and let children play.

Extension ideas

- Set up a rope trail leading to the picnic site that the children have to follow, either with their eyes open or wearing a blindfold. This will add to the excitement of getting to the site and finding out what is happening.
- Provide water and food colouring to make drinks for the picnic.
- Do some real baking beforehand with the children, taking the results outside for everyone to enjoy.
- Allow the children to eat their lunch outside with the bears.

Reflections

At the end of the picnic, ask the children to tell their bear the best thing they did during the session. This bear then tells another bear, and so on round the group. If some children find it hard to talk to others or share their thoughts, this can be a good way of enabling them to do so with less pressure. You could ask the bears what they enjoyed, directing them to tell the children, who can then tell you!

Links to EYFS

- Personal, social and emotional development: Making relationships (ELG 08).

Goldilocks and the Three Bears

Stories are a fantastic way to engage children with learning outdoors. Traditional tales are particularly well structured for telling outside. As well as this, they are usually familiar to children, who will find these stories easy to retell.

Starter

Introduce the story of the three bears and Goldilocks, asking the children if they know it. Perhaps they can identify characters or events. Having set the scene, go on a three bears scavenger hunt, looking for objects to represent elements from the story: something that looks like Goldilocks' long blond hair, or three different-sized objects to represent the bears. You may want to create a scavenger sheet with pictures of the objects to collect.

Resources

• Short length of rope
• Sticky-backed googly eyes
• Collected natural items.

Main activity

Form a circle and prepare to tell the story in full. To do so, the children need to find items from the story to create a visual story line. If these items have not been collected earlier, start by asking a group of children to collect four natural objects, one to represent each bear and one for Goldilocks. It can help to stick some googly eyes on the objects to bring them to life.

If you can, tell the story from memory, using eye contact, facial expression and different tones of voice. This may take some practice, but it is much more engaging than using the same old picture book again!

Lay a short piece of rope on the ground to illustrate the story's timeline. As you tell the story, add found items to represent key elements, such as the bowls, spoons, chairs and beds. Move the characters along the line to represent the way the story progresses, making sure you involve the children.

Extension ideas

• Give the children lengths of rope so that they can make their own story lines for this story or another traditional tale.
• Use the story as a basis for imaginative play, introducing teddy bears and asking the children to make homes for them.
• Make a ground picture using natural materials to illustrate a part of the story, for example, the three bears' house.
• Use porridge oats in your mud kitchen or messy-play area, providing bowls, spoons and water so that the children can make their own 'porridge'. Remind them not to eat it.

Reflections

Use a teddy bear as a means of gathering the children's views on the activity. Children who find it difficult to speak in a group may be more comfortable talking to the bear.

The learning can be followed up indoors, with play in a home corner or another imaginative play area based on the story. Provide plenty of opportunities to listen to and retell the story.

Links to EYFS

• Understanding of the world: People and communities (ELG 13)
• Expressive arts and design: Being imaginative (ELG 17).

Traditional tales have been fascinating children with their mix of excitement, trepidation and repetition for hundreds of years. Tell these familiar tales outdoors to deepen the children's understanding of the structure of a good story. Provide lots of opportunities for them to be retold in different forms.

Starter

Once the children know the story, play Sleeping Troll. Form a circle and ask an adult or child to stand in the middle wearing a blindfold and guard some 'treasure': a bell or bunch of keys. When ready, pick a child, who must attempt to sneak into the circle and steal the troll's treasure without waking him/her up. If the troll hears them approaching, they must point at the place where they think the thief is. If they are correct, pick another child to try. If the troll is incorrect, the thief continues until caught or successful. Change the troll regularly.

Resources

• Blue material to represent a river
• Crates
• Tyres
• Planks
• Logs
• Wood slices
• Stones.

Main activity

Start by telling the story, which can be done in a variety of ways. You could read the story from a book, tell it from memory, ask the children to help out with familiar parts, or make a story line with collected objects.

Once familiar with the story, discuss its key elements and what makes it exciting. Explain that the children are going to make some bridges like the one in the story. Place blue material on the ground to represent the river. Challenge the children to make a bridge over it so the three goats can cross to the other side safely. You will need to provide some loose parts to enable this to happen (see the list above). If you have any water on your site, you could create a real stream to try to cross!

Extension ideas

• Build a wobbly bridge for the children to balance on. Tie parallel ropes between sturdy trees. Challenge the children to cross by standing on the lower rope and holding on to the higher one. How many will fall in and get chased by the grumpy troll?
• Make troll faces on the trees using clay or mud, decorating them with collected materials.
• Make miniature bridges for small world characters from the story.

Reflections

Use the story to explore such questions as the following:
• How do you think the Billy Goats felt as they were crossing the river?
• How did the troll feel?
• Do they think the troll was right or wrong to want to eat the Billy Goats?
• What do you feel about the ending of the story?

Discussions like this help to explore complex emotions, as well as considering moral choices.

Links to EYFS

• Understanding of the world: People and communities (ELG 13)
• Expressive arts and design: Being imaginative (ELG 17).

The Three Little Pigs

This is another traditional tale that provides lots of exciting opportunities for learning and play. Think about when you do this activity as it is more pleasant to work with water and sand in warmer weather.

Starter
Tell this tale using the story line technique from page 45 or with simple puppets. Involve the children by asking them to find objects in your outdoor space to indicate different parts of the story. For example, items to represent the building materials that the three pigs use.

Resources
• Straw
• Sticks
• Bricks or stones
• Sand
• Water
• Trowels
• Buckets or baskets
• Spades.

Main activity
After telling the story, ask the children if they can remember the different building materials the pigs used. Once these have been identified, and if you have not previously done so, ask the children to find something to represent each of the materials: straw, sticks and bricks. You may need to take some straw or stones with you, depending on your site. Collect the materials in buckets or baskets.

After they have explored the space, gather all the children's finds, adding any you have brought with you. Give the children the opportunity to build houses for the pigs as follows.

Straw
Combine dry grass, straw or other thin material with water and mud. If you get the consistency right, you will produce a material called cob, which has been used for building for thousands of years. The children can shape and form the cob into blocks or other shapes to form their houses.

Sticks
Use sticks pushed into the ground or formed into bundles using elastic bands. You can cover the resultant stick structures with leaves or straw to make the roofs.

Bricks
Bring bricks to your outdoor area or use stones from it to make little houses. Sand and water make an excellent cement. The children can use trowels and spoons to manipulate the mixture and stick their bricks together to build a real wall!

Extension ideas
• Add straw, sticks, stones and sand to your mud kitchen or small world area for free-play.
• Once the children have had a go at building their houses, challenge them to retell parts of the story using them as the setting.
• Add different building materials, such as wooden blocks/off cuts and similar, for the children to build with.
• Use large, old cardboard boxes so that the children can build houses big enough to accommodate themselves.

Reflections
Visit each house, giving each group an opportunity to tell you how they made it and how they feel about the experience. When sat in a circle, pass a talking stick around it so the children all have a chance to talk about the session if they want to.

Links to EYFS
• Understanding of the world: People and communities (ELG 13)
• Expressive arts and design: Being imaginative (ELG 17).

The Gingerbread Man

This is another traditional tale that is popular with children and provides lots of potential for outdoor learning. Children love the repetition in this story, as well as the thrill of knowing what is coming at the end!

Starter
Play Hide and Seek. Once the children have played a few rounds, change the rules by telling them that they are now going to look for the gingerbread man, who is hiding nearby. Ask an assistant to hide a gingerbread man puppet or a laminated picture of a gingerbread man, while you and the children close your eyes and count to 20. Whoever finds the gingerbread man is allowed to hide him for the next round.

Resources
• Gingerbread Man story
• Clay or mud
• Wooden boards
• Rolling pins
• Gingerbread man biscuit cutters
• Dressing-up clothes.

Main activity
Involve the children in telling the story of the gingerbread man, using natural materials as props. You could use a puppet or an object from your outdoor setting for each character: a stick for the old woman, a pine cone for the dog and an orange leaf for the cunning fox.

Dig some mud or clay from your site and use it to make your own gingerbread men. If none is available, bring some with you. Allow each child to roll out their clay on a board with a small rolling pin, before using one of the biscuit cutters to create their own gingerbread man. Ask the children to gather materials for the eyes, mouth and clothes, making each gingerbread man unique. When finished, you could ask the children to act out the story using their newly-baked gingerbread men, or provide dressing-up clothes to do the same.

Challenge the children to build homes for the gingerbread men from gathered materials that will keep them safe from the clever fox.

Extension ideas
• Cut out gingerbread man templates from card and stick natural materials on them as decoration.
• Go on a gingerbread man treasure hunt. Place clues around the site that lead to where the gingerbread man is hiding. Help the children to get started and observe to see if they can follow the clues to find him.
• Make a story sack with key characters and props from the story to be used outdoors to encourage imaginative play.

Reflections
As with all traditional tales, there is an element of fear in this story. Use this to stimulate a discussion about feelings and emotions. How do you think the gingerbread man felt at different parts of the story? What about the old woman or the fox? Do you think the fox was wrong to eat the gingerbread man? What about if he was really hungry? All stories can be used as a starting point for discussion about moral decisions and making good choices. Make sure you listen to the children's opinions and do not use this time as an opportunity to impose your own!

Links to EYFS
• Understanding of the world: People and communities (ELG 13)
• Expressive arts and design: Being imaginative (ELG 17).

We're Going on a Bear Hunt

We're Going on a Bear Hunt by Michael Rosen and Helen Oxenbury is another brilliant story for outdoor play. The language is simple and repetitive, so children can quickly become familiar with the story. As it is mostly set outdoors, the narrative can be explored physically.

Starter
Set the scene so you can lead the children on a bear hunt, once they are familiar with the story. Here are some suggestions for different areas:
• Long, wavy grass: if you do not have any, find a source of dried grass.
• Deep, cold river: a natural puddle or a shallow tray full of water.
• Thick, oozy mud: a muddy puddle or some soil mixed with water.
• Deep, dark forest: a tree or wooded area. Alternatively, scatter twigs on the ground.
• Swirling, whirling snowstorm – a tray full of flour. Sprinkle some on the children's heads as they walk through it.
• Dark, gloomy cave: make one using some rocks or find a natural enclosed area.

Once you have found the bear, make your way back to the beginning.

Resources
• Spades and trowels
• Jugs/buckets/cups/spoons/watering cans
• Mud
• Digging tools.

Main activity
Allow the children to play with the materials once your bear hunt is over. You could provide the children with some of the resources above.

Discuss the bear's home. Why did it live in a cave? Where else might it live? Provide a range of materials for the children to make their ideas into reality. Prompt as required. Allow time for the children to explain what they have made to the rest of the group.

Extension ideas
• Make bears from clay, using natural materials for the arms, legs and face.
• Draw or sculpt a friend for the bear.

• Make a sticky collection of items from the stages of the journey using double-sided tape on a piece of card.

Reflections
The sadness of the bear at the end of the story provides an opportunity for the children to talk about times when they felt sad or lonely. Explore how they would help the bear think of practical strategies to help manage these emotions.

Links to EYFS
• Expressive arts and design: Being imaginative (ELG 17).

The Gruffalo

Stories can be an excellent introduction to an outdoor session and can really capture children's imagination when told outside. Using a familiar story is good for children's sense of security if the environment is unfamiliar.

Starter
Read *The Gruffalo* by Julia Donaldson and Axel Scheffler with the children, searching the illustrations for the woodland animals mentioned in the text. Discuss the story using questions such as the following.
• Did you notice any animals?
• Which ones did you see?
• Where might the animals live?
• What can you tell me about the animal homes in the story?

Once you have finished, go on a hunt around your outdoor area looking for evidence of animal homes. You may find a hole where a mouse might live or a pile of logs that could be a home for a beetle or woodlouse. Look for birds' nests too. Ask the children for their ideas as well and allow time for discussion.

Resources
• Woodland soft toys
• Collected materials.

Main activity
Take some woodland soft toys outside with you. If you can find the animals from the story, even better! Introduce the children to the animals and explain that they need some friends to build them a home as they are out in the cold with nowhere to live. Share some ideas on how to use twigs, leaves, feathers, stones and other gathered materials to make simple homes for the animals. Invite the children to make their own. If your site does not have many natural resources, you may need to bring some with you.

Ask the children to think about what their own homes provide them with, such as safety, shelter and warmth. Ask them to create homes for the animals that reflect these elements. Once the homes are complete, the children could extend them by adding a garden, a dining area or, even, a swimming pool.

Extension ideas
Show the children how to make Gruffalo faces on tree trunks using mud and gathered materials. Can they remember all the features of the Gruffalo?

Use paper plates and double-sided tape to make masks based on the mouse in the story. The children could use gathered materials to decorate the masks and then use them to act out the story.

Reflections
Use a puppet or soft toy to visit the homes the children have made and ask them questions about their work. The puppet could point out things he/she likes about the homes, or you could ask the rest of the children to explain what they like about each other's homes. It is important for children to have the opportunity to talk about what they have made, so do not rush this part.

Links to EYFS
• Expressive arts and design: Being imaginative (ELG 17).

Stick Man

Stick Man is a well-loved picture book by Julia Donaldson and Axel Scheffler that is ideal for sharing outdoors. The story will fuel children's imaginations, helping them to visualise a simple stick in a host of different guises.

Make sure you have plenty of sticks available before starting this activity, including one to represent Stick Man.

Starter

Start by reading the story. If the children are familiar with it, they can join in with the repetition and share their ideas about what might happen next.

Go on a Stick Man adventure around your site. You could hide your Stick Man and challenge the children to find him, or visit the different places in the story together, real or imagined, depending on your site. Ask the children to repeat the relevant part of the story at each place. You might want to use pictures from the story in different areas of your outdoor space to remind the children of its sequence.

Resources

• Sticks
• Clay
• Elastic bands
• Googley eyes.

Main activity

Challenge the children to make a Stick Man each and find him somewhere to live. They will need to find a stick that is the right body shape. If this is tricky, elastic bands can be used to join sticks to make arms and legs. The children could stick googley eyes on their stick and/or draw a face on it to bring their Stick Man to life.

Ask the children to find a tree in your setting that looks like the family's tree from the story. Challenge some of the children to re-enact Stick Man's journey back to his tree; others to decorate the tree to make it a suitable home; and others to make the rest of Stick Man's family. They could use clay to join the sticks together, decorating the figures with buttons and bits of material.

Extension ideas

• Ask the children what else a stick could be: a pirate sword, a boat for a fairy, and so on.
• Paint sticks with bright poster paint and use them for Hide and Seek.
• Make some of the other things from the book, such as simple bows and arrows or swords, remembering to talk about how to use these safely.
• Make a story line on the ground with rope and illustrate the different parts of the story along it using natural materials.

Reflections

Stick Man was mistaken for lots of other things in the story. Ask the children to imagine being something else. What would they be and why? Use a digital camera to record the children's thoughts for a video diary.

Links to EYFS

• Mathematics: Shape, space and measures (ELG 12)
• Expressive arts and design: Being imaginative (ELG 17).

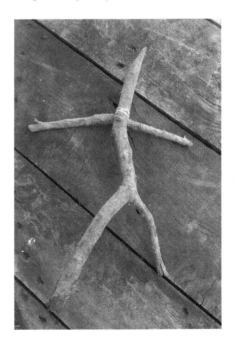

Easter outside

As the days start to get longer and signs of spring are appearing, the natural world begins to come back to life. Use this magical time of the year to explore the outdoors, looking for signs of new life and the changing of the seasons.

Starter

Explore your outdoor area for spring changes: plant growth, buds on trees, flowers coming through, birds nesting and rising temperatures. Ask the children to share the changes they notice. This is a good opportunity to talk about respecting the natural world and nurturing new life. For example, should we encourage the picking of spring flowers or leave them for others to enjoy?

Take a camera with you to photograph the things that should be left where you found them.

Resources
• Chocolate eggs
• Easter chicks
• Wool
• String
• Straw
• Sticks.

Main activity

During the Easter period, take the children on an egg hunt. Hide small wrapped chocolate eggs around your outdoor area before the session. It may help to hide them in small baskets or containers to keep them clean.

Send the children off to hunt for the eggs. Each time a child finds an egg, they must bring it to you. Once all the eggs have been found, share them out to ensure everyone gets an equal amount.

Talk about the ways in which birds construct nests before asking the children to build their own for their chocolate eggs or other substitutes. Provide nest-making materials, such as wool, string, straw and sticks.

They could also make Easter chicks using natural materials.

Extension ideas
• Make mini-nests out of paper muffin cases to hold small chocolate eggs that can be taken home.
• Draw a map of your outdoor area and ask the children to mark on it where they found their eggs during the hunt.
• Use mud or clay to make an Easter chick, pressing leaves into it for feathers.
• Link the above activities with those on birds' nest on page 20.

Reflections

Hunting for eggs is a very physical activity, so the children might need some quiet time at the end of the session to calm down and reflect. Collect a basketful of interesting natural objects: stones, feathers, shells, pine cones, and so on. Invite each child to choose an object that interests them and find a quiet place to sit with it. Ask them to spend some time using their senses, excluding taste, to explore it. How does it feel, smell and sound? What does it look like? This is a good exercise to encourage mindfulness and relaxation, as well as calming a group before returning indoors. After a period of quiet, ask the group to share their experiences.

Links to EYFS
• Understanding of the world: People and communities (ELG 13).

Autumn leaves

This activity introduces children to autumn colours and explores the changes that take place in this beautiful season. Autumn is a magical time of year to be out in nature and provides a great opportunity for lots of outdoor learning.

Starter
Talk about the wonder of nature with the children, discussing what changes appear magical. Ask the children to close their eyes and listen. Every time they hear a new sound, ask them to grab it with their hand and store it to listen to later. This is a great way to encourage children to talk about their sensory experiences. If your site is quiet, they may even be able to hear the leaves falling!

If there are leaves falling, look at them together. Challenge the children to catch a falling leaf. Anyone who does so is allowed to make a wish!

Resources
• Thin sticks
• Colourful autumn leaves
• Baskets or bags for collecting
• Masking tape
• Elastic bands.

Main activity
Ask each child to collect a big armful of leaves. Encourage them to notice the leaves' colours and shapes. You can use baskets or bags to make collecting easier.

Use open questions to extend the learning:
• What do the leaves feel like between your fingers?
• What sounds did the leaves make as you collected them?
• What do you imagine the leaves are feeling at this time of change?

Each child needs to find a thin stick, which will become their autumn magic wand. Once the children have what they need, they use masking tape or an elastic band to fix their leaves to the tip of their stick to create a wand.

This is ideal for developing fine-motor skills, although very young children may need a little help. For a simpler version of a wand, push the stick through the leaves creating a leaf kebab!

Once all the children have made their wands, do some magic together! Make up a spell to conjure up some autumn enchantments.

Extension ideas
• Add other items to the wands, such as feathers or long stems of grass.
• Decorate the stick using coloured insulation tape or paint.
• Ask the children to create a group spell. Write it down so you have a record of it.
• Ask the children, 'If you could cast any magic spell, what would it be?'

Reflections
Ask the children to find a favourite leaf and describe it to the group, including why they chose it.
• How does your leaf reflect your time outdoors today?

Invite each child to swap their leaf with someone else's.
• What are the similarities and differences between the leaves?
• Which leaves would be friends?
• Which leaf best reflects your personality?

Links to EYFS
• Physical Development: Moving and Handling (ELG 04)
• Understanding the World: The World (ELG 13).

Bonfire Night

 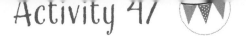

Activities linked to specific dates or times of the year are a good way to deepen children's learning and explore familiar events. Bonfire Night lends itself wonderfully to outdoor learning as it encompasses cold days, fires and, of course, fireworks!

If you do not celebrate Bonfire Night, there are many other festivals that involve fireworks, which the activities below can be adapted for.

Starter
Talk with the children about Bonfire Night, carrying out a knowledge harvest by asking questions such as:
• Who has seen a real fire before?
• How did it make you feel?
• Has anyone been to a firework display?
• What do you remember about it?

Explain to the children that they are going to make some fireworks of their own. These will be leaf-fireworks! Send the group off to collect some brightly-coloured leaves from the ground of the setting. Ask them to look out for firework colours: reds, yellows and oranges. Encourage the children to lay their leaves out on a piece of black card to make a firework pattern. Experiment with different shapes and sizes, using bigger pieces of card to create a sky full of exploding fireworks. On a windy day, you may need to use double-sided tape to stick the leaves to.

Resources
• Sticks
• Red, yellow and orange tissue paper
• Paper plates.

Main activity
Another important part of Bonfire Night is, of course, the bonfire. Although lighting a real fire is best left to an appropriately-trained person, you can make pretend fires using sticks and coloured tissue paper to represent the flames. Give the children some red, yellow and orange tissue paper and ask them to gather some sticks to build a pretend fire where they think it would be safe and useful. This might be near a den or a special

place, and can lead to lots of imaginative play. You might want to provide paper plates and ask them to cook some delicious pretend food for a Bonfire Night treat!

Extension ideas
• Invite a trained adult to light a real fire and cook something on it. Talk about the sights, sounds and smells of this experience.
• Use biodegradable glitter to add a touch of sparkle to the children's leaf firework pictures.
• Laminate the leaf fireworks to make them more durable and use them for a display.

Reflections
Sitting round a fire is a great way to reflect as it brings everyone together and provides a focal point, which allows the children to talk without too much pressure. If you do not have a real fire, recreate one as outlined above and sit round it to share your thoughts about the session. To make it even more realistic, ask the children to close their eyes and imagine the smells, sounds and feelings of sitting round a real fire. How does it feel?

Links to EYFS
• Expressive arts and design: Exploring and using media and materials (ELG 16).

Winter badges

> Winter is a great time to get outside and explore the natural world. Make sure the children are wrapped up warm before you venture out.

Starter

Children need to keep moving in order to stay warm when outdoors in the cold. Play physical games to help with this, such as Winter Wanderers. Ask the children to run around the outside space imitating swirling snowflakes, spinning and whirling as they move. When you blow a whistle, the children must freeze, each holding a pose as if a statue made of ice. Who can stay still for the longest?

Resources

- Card
- String
- Double-sided tape (carpet tape works well)
- Charcoal.

Main activity

In order to make winter badges, some preparation is needed.

Take a small piece of card, attach a loop of string to the back of it and stick a piece of double-sided tape to the front. Make one for each child and adult taking part.

Challenge the children to create their own winter badge by sticking found outdoor items onto their badge's tape. For an extra challenge, ask the children to collect specific types of objects, such as things with interesting smells, textures or colours.

Ask the children about the things they have found, discussing how the badges would look different if created in the summer.

Extension ideas

- Draw on the badge using charcoal, instead of sticking things on a strip of tape.
- Carry out this activity at different times of the year, comparing the results.
- Take photographs of the seasonal collections and use them to make a display about the natural yearly cycle.

- Add a range of collected items to some plastic trays full of water. Leave the trays outside overnight to freeze, investigating any changes in the morning. It is exciting to take the trays indoors and watch the water melt, releasing the objects.
- Encourage the children to watch their breath condense in the cold air, and talk about what they notice.

Reflections

On a really cold day, take the children outside and wrap them in blankets, creating cosy nests. Ask the children to describe how it feels to be wrapped up warm when the weather is cold.

You can give the children cameras or iPads to take photographs of natural objects that interest them. Invite them to tell the rest of the group why they chose a particular object.

Links to EYFS

- Understanding the world: The world (ELG 14).

Christmas outdoors

There are so many lovely festive artefacts that can be made outdoors by children using natural materials. These can be taken home as wonderful alternatives to the usual glittery Christmas cards and paper snowflakes.

Starter

Go on a Christmas scavenger hunt with the children around your outdoor area. Look for things that are associated with Christmas and photograph or collect them as appropriate for an indoor display. Some of the following work well:
• A robin
• Some ice or frost
• A stick shaped like reindeer antlers
• Holly berries
• A tree that looks like a Christmas tree
• Something to wrap up as a present
• A snow (or mud!) man
• Mistletoe.

Resources

• Pine cones
• String
• Glue
• Biodegradable glitter
• Sequins

• Washable pens
• Log slices, each with a pre-drilled hole
• Small sprigs of greenery
• 15cm lengths of evergreen foliage
• Leaves in a range of colours.

Main activity

Below is a selection of Christmas crafts to try. Make sure anything you suggest is age appropriate and can be made by a child independently or with a small amount of adult support.
• Pine-cone baubles – Glue biodegradable glitter and sequins onto large pine cones and hang them from string to make Christmas decorations.
• Christmas-tree table decorations – Cut thin log slices or buy a set from a supplier. Drill a small hole in each base and push the end of an evergreen branch into it to make a Christmas tree. Children can decorate these with biodegradable glitter and sequins, using pens to add colour.
• Elder candles – Use a butter knife to strip the bark from an elder stick, inserting a coloured leaf into one end of it to create an elder candle.

Extension ideas

• Natural Christmas cards – Stick a pressed fern leaf onto the front of a folded piece of card. Decorate with biodegradable glitter.
• Put some reindeer food out just before Christmas and see if it gets eaten, and by what.
• With a trained practitioner, light a campfire and have a Christmas feast outdoors.
• Sing Christmas songs outdoors.

Reflections

Christmas is a time for giving as well as receiving. Ask the children to think of a part of the outdoor area or a natural object in it that they would like to give a gift to as a thank you. Gather some pretty stones, glass beads or other treasures, letting each child choose one they like, which they wrap in some tissue paper. They can then go and say thank you to their special place or object and leave the gift until the end of the Christmas season.

Links to EYFS

• Understanding the world: People and communities (ELG 13).

Quiet time

Times of quiet reflection are built into all of the activities in this book, but it can be beneficial to devote a whole session to this practice. This may be at the end of a term or on an occasion when you have a smaller group. Make the most of these opportunities for stillness by really tuning in to the natural world.

Starter

Give each child a mat or carpet tile and ask them to sit on it for a few moments in a quiet spot in your outdoor area that is special to them. This is an opportunity to notice what is around them. If this is a struggle, give them some prompts to help. Ask them to return to their senses if they become distracted. What can they hear, see, smell or touch? Encourage them to pick up a nearby object and examine it in detail, looking at the colours and shapes, feeling the texture. You could try using blindfolds to help the children focus on their non-visual senses. It is not recommended to ask children to sit for too long on a very cold day.

Resources
• Plenty of leaves.

Main activity

Talk with the children about their experiences. How easy or hard did they find it to sit silently and observe? Explain that for the next activity, they need to be very quiet and still as they are going to become part of the natural environment. Ask for a volunteer who is willing to lie down and be covered with leaves, with their head remaining free. Once they know what to do, ask the children to work in pairs, taking it in turns to cover each other with leaves. Assist as necessary. When one of each pair is covered, allow them time to lie and appreciate all that is around them. Can they see the treetops swaying in the breeze or hear the rustling of the leaves? When the time is up, pairs swap so that everyone has a turn to become part of the ground.

Some children might be nervous about this activity, so be sensitive.

Extension ideas
• Try this activity at different times of the year to see how the experience differs.
• Record these experiences using a digital camera, creating a video diary of your site and the seasonal changes it experiences.

• Make an outline of a child with leaves and ask them to fill it in with natural materials.
• Sit under a tarpaulin when it is raining and listen to the sounds the rain makes.

Reflections

This activity is about quiet reflection, so to end you could do something more physical. Lay a long line of rope on the ground and challenge the children to walk along it without falling off. Imagine it is a high wire! As they walk, ask them to think about what they have enjoyed about the session and, when they get to the end of the line, shout it out!

Younger children may need someone to hold their hand during this activity.

Links to EYFS
• Personal, social and emotional development: Managing feelings and behaviour (ELG 07)

Builder's Tray
50 Exciting Ways to Use a Builder's Tray
978-1-903670-15-6

Let's Take a Story Book Outside
Exciting Ways to Promote Outdoor Creativity
978-1-903670-76-7

Let's Talk Behaviour!
50 Inclusive Ideas to Support Effective Communication and Understanding
978-1-903670-93-4

Literacy Outdoors
50 Exciting Starting Points for Outdoor Literacy Experiences
978-903670-53-8

Maths Outdoors
50 Exciting Ways to Develop Mathematical Awareness Outdoors
978-1-903670-61-3

Mud Kitchens and Beyond
50 Exciting Ideas for Investigative Play 978-1-903670-96-5

Science Outdoors
50 Exciting Ways for Children to Explore the World Around Them
978-1-903670-67-5

This is the Way I Like to Play
50 Exciting Ideas to Support Investigative Play through Schemas
978-1-903670-95-8

We're OK with Risky Play
50 Exciting Ideas to Build Resilience and Self-confidence
978-1-903670-99-6

Other relevant publications include:

Let's Get Talking!
Exciting Ways to Help Children with Speech and Language Difficulties
978-1-903670-88-0

Let's Talk About Maths!
Exciting Ways to Develop Children's Language and Love of Maths From an Early Age
978-1-903670-92-7

On Your Marks!
A Practical Guide to Mark Making, Early Writing and Language
978-1-903670-97-2

Supporting Quiet Children
Exciting Ideas and Activities to Help 'Reluctant Talkers' Become 'Confident Talkers'
978-1-903670-90-3

Adventures Outdoors: Mud
YD0418

Adventures Outdoors: Wind
YD0419

Adventures Outdoors: Puddles
YD0420

For further details about these and other exciting products, visit our website:
www.yellow-door.net